FROMMER'S

HOW TO BEAT THE HIGH COST OF TRAVEL

by Tom Brosnahan

1982-1983 Edition

Published by Frommer/Pasmantier Publishers
A Simon & Schuster Division of
Gulf & Western Corporation
1230 Avenue of the Americas
New York, NY 10020

ISBN 0-671-43845-X

Manufactured in the United States of America

Design by Stanley S. Drate/Folio Graphics Co., Inc.

*Although every effort was made to ensure the accuracy
of prices and the travel information appearing in this
book, it should be kept in mind that prices can and do
fluctuate in the course of time and so also do the various
factors affecting the travel industry.*

Contents

Introduction

Travel is one of life's greatest adventures, and no potential traveler should sit home because the cost of a trip looks high. People have always had the urge to travel, to refresh their minds and bodies with experiences in different settings, among new faces, with varying climates and customs. Don't let fear of the finances take away that right to enjoy these experiences.

Only a few years ago, travel was incredibly cheap. The post-war economy was favorable to the dollar, and North Americans could travel to Europe, the Middle East, South America, and even the Orient and spend only $5 a day. But the world economy has changed. Today, the pubs of London ring in summer with American voices recalling the days when bed and breakfast right in the heart of the city was theirs for $3. In those halcyon days, a pub lunch cost 70¢, beer included. Usually such reminiscences are followed quickly by horror stories about today's prices: the $200 hotel room, the $90 dinner, the $60 bill for drinks at a nightclub. The unspoken conclusion is that the great days of travel are gone, never to return.

Nothing could be further from the truth. America's victory in World War II, coupled with the development of efficient air transport, opened the world to an entire generation of North Americans. For more than a decade, we could afford to be as careless with our travel dollars as we were with our energy resources. But now the price of travel has gone up along with the price of energy.

What can be done? Well, a glance at the solutions to the energy crisis will serve as inspiration: people are staying just as warm, driving just as far, and doing just as much work as before, but they are using much, much less energy—and they love it! The "crisis" has forced us all to think, to create, to be ingenious and self-sufficient. Everyone is proud of saving energy and using it more wisely. Everyone wonders how we could have wasted such valuable resources in earlier times.

Just as the answer to higher heating bills is more insulation, and the answer to higher gasoline bills is more fuel-efficient cars, the answer to higher travel costs is not to stay at home, but to search out ways to travel more efficiently and cost-effectively.

SOME AMUSING HISTORICAL PRECEDENTS

To prove that you needn't stay at home when there's a whole world to explore, here are some inspiring tales from the exploits of early cost-conscious travelers:

- The Patriarch Abraham doesn't seem to have had much trouble traveling all over the Middle East: Iraq, Syria, Lebanon, Jordan, Israel, Egypt. This was around 2000 B.C.

- Alexander the Great, ambitious and bored at home, took off to see new sights. In the fourth century B.C., he toured Greece, Turkey, Syria, Iraq, Iran,

Jordan, Lebanon, Israel, Egypt. Then he went to India, which he liked, and discovered the Indian Ocean, which he liked even more. He died in Babylon at the age of 33, a well-traveled fellow.

● The Romans gave Hannibal (a Carthaginian) trouble about a visa, so instead of simply hopping across the straits from Tunisia to Sicily, he took the scenic route through Algeria, Morocco, Spain, France and Switzerland, in 218 B.C.

● In 1241, the Great Khan of the Mongols died in Ulan Bator, Mongolia. His sons were away in Hungary, conquering it and getting to know Europe, but when they heard Dad had died, they all went back to Ulan Bator (6000 miles away) to divide the inheritance.

● Marco Polo has gained an ageless reputation as an intrepid traveler—he began as an Italian businessman living in Istanbul. When the travel bug bit him in 1260, he took a trip to southern Russia. He enjoyed himself so much that he went farther, to Bukhara in Turkestan. Along the way he met some travelers going to China, and their trip presented an opportunity he couldn't ignore. When he got to Peking, he talked to the emperor, who asked him about getting Western medical and technical help. Marco hiked back to Europe, went to Rome, and put the emperor's request to the Pope. His Holiness wasn't enthusiastic, so Marco started back to China to report to his friend, the emperor. On this trip, he took his sons ("It'll be good for you!"). Marco liked China so much that he got a job there and stayed a while.

● Hernando de Soto, a Spanish real estate speculator, landed in Florida in 1539, presaging the Florida land boom of later centuries. Without roads it was tough for Hernando to find his way around, but he still managed some side trips, touring Georgia, Alabama, Arkansas, Oklahoma and Mississippi. He never did get his land in Florida.

● In more recent times, thrifty travelers have sailed around the world in little boats, ridden bicycles across North America, or journeyed through five continents on motorcycles.

These notable trips are mentioned only half in jest. The point is simple: people have always traveled, and they always will. The world was not frighteningly huge and expensive to the medieval European monk who wanted to see Jerusalem. If he wanted to go, he went. So can you.

ABOUT THIS BOOK

This is not merely a book of travel tips, though there is much detailed and immediately useful data contained in it. More important than the information on guest houses, discount airfares, and free travelers checks are the mental exercises and thought patterns that you can learn by using this book.

Like all other pursuits, travel is a task to be mastered. With experience, one learns how to do it most easily, pleasurably, and cost-effectively. To get the most out of this book, look upon it as a training course in successful travel, taught not just by one experienced travel professional, but by dozens of master travelers. Besides my own ideas and experiences gathered over the years, I have benefited from the wisdom of many other professionals. The experiences of thousands of other travelers, who read and use my guidebooks and write to me about their experiences, have immeasurably enriched my own body of experience.

All of us have had the experience of laboring at some seemingly difficult task. A master of the trade comes along, and with a few words of advice or suggestion opens up vast new fields of possibilities, cuts the work load in half, or shortens the time by a third. "Why didn't I think of that?" we say to ourselves. "Here I am, spending hours delicately peeling tiny shreds of skin off this tomato, when a few seconds' parboiling would have accomplished the task much better!"

Get a Copy of This Book Free

For many years, Frommer/Pasmantier guides have benefited from the sage advice and keen travel savvy of readers. Thousands of our readers have written describing their travels, and contributing specific money-saving tips which they wanted to communicate to other readers. The guidebooks have become true clearinghouses for a wealth of cost-cutting information gathered by tens of thousands of travelers.

The editors at Frommer/Pasmantier recognize what a valuable service these "Readers' Suggestions" provide to our far-flung readership, and so in gratitude they send out free copies of the new edition of each book, hot off the press, to those readers whose suggestions have been printed in each book.

Though *How To Beat the High Cost of Travel* is not strictly speaking a guidebook, we'd like to give you the same opportunity to help other readers, appear in print, and receive a free copy of the next edition of this book. Send your suggestions, tips, and strategies to me, Tom Brosnahan, Frommer/Pasmantier Publishers, Simon & Schuster Building, 1230 Avenue of the Americas, New York, NY 10020. I'll read each letter personally, send you a reply if possible, and consider your suggestions for inclusion in the updated edition. I sincerely enjoy reading letters from other travelers, so I hope you'll give me—and other readers—the benefits of your experience.

Finding the easier, or quicker, or less expensive way doesn't require genius. What's required is creativity, ingenuity, clear sight, and a willingness to explore new possibilities. Here are some principles to help you develop those skills.

1

The Principles of Cost-Effective Travel

Let's get down to specifics—theoretical specifics, that is. Exactly how can one go about exploiting the possibilities for reduced costs? How do I get more, and better, travel for my money, regardless of how much I spend? Here are four important principles, or "Laws," followed by detailed explanations of each.

1. Don't take "no" for an answer until you're sure the answer is "no."
2. Search for the Point of Mutual Advantage.
3. Look beyond the Obvious.
4. Commitment saves money; flexibility usually costs money.

THE FIRST LAW

Don't take "no" for an answer until you're sure the answer is "no." Most of us will accept a "no" without question: Do you have this in stock? Is there a cheaper flight? You have no rooms available at all? In lots and lots of situations, the "no" has nothing to do with reality, but rather with the personal preferences of the one answering "no." "No, we don't have it" can mean, "I don't feel like going to look for it." And "No, we have no rooms at all" can mean "We've got a few rooms, but I don't want to rent one to a single traveler—I want to get the double rate."

Your job, in obeying this Law, is to discover the true significance of the negative answer. Get more information, don't just walk away. This is actually quite easy, and not unpleasant. No need to threaten or berate, just persist. At the point when you would normally turn and walk away, force yourself to stay and ask a few more questions. What can it hurt?

"You must have something similar or interchangeable in stock."

"Perhaps there has been a cancellation or a no-show, and a room is free."

"Maybe if I come back just before flight time there will be a seat open."

By persisting, you'll demonstrate to the other person that it will be easier to satisfy you than to get rid of you by saying "no." This Law works. It works at home and it works abroad.

"But I've tried that," you say, "and it has never produced anything for me." Nonsense. Notice that you are supposed to stick like glue "at the point when you would normally turn and walk away." This means that there will be some tension in the situation, because the other person will have expected you to go away. You'll feel uncomfortable; if there are people in line behind you, they'll start to fidget. The person you're asking will feel uncomfortable, and to get rid of that discomfort will try to solve your problem.

Over half the time, it will solve your problem right then and there: you will find the thing you want, or that elusive charter flight, or that spare room. How can you be sure when the answer really is "no"? Simple: the other person will show a bit of annoyance, which contains the message, "Now I really *have* done all I can; I can't help you, and you won't go away, so I'm annoyed." When this point comes, clear the air with a kind word such as, "I really appreciate your efforts and that second look." You haven't been pushy or impolite, just persistent.

THE SECOND LAW

Search constantly for the Point of Mutual Advantage. The Point of Mutual Advantage is that point where the interests of the buyer and the seller come together, and both make out well. The clearest example is a partly filled hotel. The clerk says a room costs $50. You only want to spend $30. The clerk knows that if the room goes empty (as it will, without you), the hotel earns $0. If you rent the room, you'll engender a few dollars' expenses: a few gallons of water, a kilowatt or so of electricity, a set of sheets to wash. The expenses are marginal, and almost any room price will exceed them. So the Point of Mutual Advantage is $30 or $35 for the room: you win and the hotel wins.

Remember, both sides must stand to gain from the arrangement, or there is no Point of Mutual Advantage.

In a curio shop in Florence, you see a painting you like, and also a little statue. You want to buy one or the other as a souvenir. Prices are marked, and the shopkeeper won't budge. It doesn't matter to you which one you buy, you like them both. Now, ask the shopkeeper for a special price *for the two items combined.* What does he gain? Two sales where there would have been only one; he takes in a slightly smaller markup on one item. What do you gain? Two lovely souvenirs for a bit more than you expected to spend, but a bargain nonetheless. It doesn't have to be in Florence. I bought two Japanese prints in San Francisco; I suggested a discount; the owner said, "But this guy's work is expensive!" He did agree to pay the sales tax himself, though. All I did was suggest it. In this case, for a small expenditure, he got himself a very satisfied customer.

The Point of Mutual Advantage is all around us, all the time. Look for it, find it, and exploit it. You're not being pushy, or ripping someone off. By definition, both sides win. But it's usually up to you to propose the deal.

THE THIRD LAW

Look beyond the Obvious. Accept it as fact: what you want exists and all you must do is locate it.

Here's an example of the Third Law: I arrived at Paris' Gare de Lyon, got off the train, and headed out to look for a meal. Now, around a major station there are always dozens of cafés and restaurants which aim to serve travelers just like me. I didn't know this area of Paris; I was hungry. The normal, obvious thing to do was to walk out the station door, spot a restaurant, enter and eat. The prices seemed high, though, so I decided to find a neighborhood place where the locals dined, not a place designed to catch travelers. I explored a few streets *behind* the obvious restaurants, and within ten minutes I found what I wanted: a small, friendly neighborhood restaurant that featured a daily business lunch. I had soup, pasta, meat and vegetables, salad, dessert and wine—all included—for the price of "steack et frites" (tough beef and French fries) in a crowded café facing the station.

Airport buses are another common subject for the Third Law. In many cases a few well-placed questions will reveal that the airport is served by a municipal bus at a fraction of the fancy airport bus price. You may have to walk to a bus stop ten minutes away (how long did you just walk down those endless airport concourses?), and the city bus may take a bit longer. But you'll probably save enough money for a fine meal, and you'll plunge immediately into the life of the city or country you are visiting.

Don't take "no" for an answer until you're
sure the answer is "no."
Search for the Point of Mutual Advantage.
Look beyond the Obvious.
Commitment saves money; flexibility
usually costs money.

Sightseeing tours are still another Third Law subject. Some sort of public transport has got to go close to your sight, and since local people use it every day, it must be relatively cheap.

Look beyond the Obvious, because the Obvious is often put there by someone who'd like to make a few extra dollars from you.

THE FOURTH LAW

Commitment saves money; flexibility usually costs money. We pride ourselves on the amount of personal freedom we enjoy. But when it comes to travel, flexibility is expensive because of the uncertainty involved. Hotels, airlines, rental car firms, and other businesses want to sell their services to you. But until you've actually paid for and used their services, they can't be positive of a sale. You might change your mind at the last moment, leaving them with nothing after weeks of planning. So these businesses heed the adage, "A bird in the hand is worth two in the bush." They'll go a long way in lowering price if you will only commit yourself to them. Here's an example.

Fulton Flyboy is a reservations executive for Aeolian Airlines. On October 23, his line has a flight from Chicago to Miami with 200 seats on it. Fulton's job is to fill those seats. It is just after the busy Labor Day weekend when we look in on Fulton in his office. He is worrying about the Chicago-to-Miami plane for October 23rd, even though it is seven weeks in the future.

"For that flight last year I had sold 180 seats at the full fare. But then at the last minute 100 people cancelled, didn't show, or traded the ticket for that of another airline. The plane flew less than half full, and even the 80 full-fare tickets didn't pay the bills. This year I'll try a different tack. I'll offer big discounts if people will only *promise* me they won't cancel, that they will show up (or at least pay), and that they won't switch to another airline. That commitment is worth losing a bit of money for; at least there won't be a repeat of last year's debacle."

Soon the ads appear: "Fly to Florida on Aeolian! 30% off if you buy and pay now!" It's a real bargain, and Florida-bound passengers respond by buying lots of seats. The offer expires three weeks before flight time, when business and last-minute travelers start booking seats. They have to pay full fare because they didn't help Fulton out in his plane-stuffing task, and because they wanted the freedom to change their minds at the last moment.

The day of the flight, Fulton is ecstatic. "Whoopee! I've sold 100 discount seats and 80 full-fare seats. I'm almost home free. Now, how to get people into those last 20 seats. . . . I know what to do! I'll offer a standby fare. Passengers who demand the last-minute flexibility of buying their ticket at the airport and walking on the plane will pay full fare; any leftover seats I'll sell off cheap to people who don't demand it—who are unwilling to pay for such flexibility." So Fulton's final passenger list was composed of 100 discount-rate passengers, 80 full-fare passengers, five full-fares who arrived breathless at the airport and simply *had to* get to Miami on that flight, and 15 standbys who were willing to take pot luck.

"That system works!" Fulton said to himself in self-congratulation. "If people will only commit themselves, I'll give them a good deal."

Airlines are an obvious example of businesses that are willing to give a discount in exchange for a commitment. If you think a minute, you'll realize that hotels, restaurants, and car rental firms have similar problems. They want to use their facilities to the fullest extent. They want as much time as possible to gather customers. And they want to be sure you'll come and patronize them. No-shows, who exercise their flexibility by deciding not to show up and pay for the promised service, cost the hotels and airlines plenty. These firms often routinely overbook, hoping they can guess correctly and match the number of no-shows with the number of overbookings to achieve an even 100% occupancy. If their guess is off, they lose money. It makes sense that they're happy when someone makes a commitment and pays in advance. Restaurants work this way, too. The very difference between table d'hôte and à la carte menus shows it. The chef is saying, "I'll plan a nice, balanced, delicious meal. It will be easier and less expensive for me to plan, buy for, and prepare this meal than it would be to prepare a hundred different meals based on diners' immediate desires. So I'll sell this table d'hôte meal a little cheaper to tempt people. People can also order from the à la carte menu; but it is more trouble and involves more expense to keep all that food on hand just in case somebody wants it, and to prepare it on a moment's notice, so the à la carte diners will have to pay more for the privilege of selecting exactly what they want at the moment."

More important than the information on guest houses, discount airfares, and free travelers checks are the mental exercises and thought patterns that you can learn by using this book.

With hotels, the Weekend Package leaps to mind as an example of the Fourth Law. "Come on Friday, Saturday, or Sunday," they say, "and we'll give you a special rate. But come on any other day and you will have to pay more." If you sacrifice the freedom to arrive any day you choose, you will be rewarded with direct cash savings. The hotel management knows that some travelers, particularly business people, will have to arrive on business days. These clients demand the right to arrive whenever they choose. "Sure," the hotel people say, "come whenever you like—but be prepared to pay." The business travelers have no choice, so they pay.

The point of the Fourth Law is not to hem you in with regulations, uncertainty, and inconvenience. It is to make you think in terms of flexibility vs. money. If a certain type of flexibility is not important to you, take it and turn it into cash, which will buy you a type of flexibility which probably will be more important to you. Book a Super-APEX flight in advance, and you'll save enough over the ordinary airfare to upgrade your hotel accommodations, or to dine luxuriously.

The aforementioned examples are straightforward and familiar. But to keep to the Fourth Law, you should combine it with the Third Law, Look beyond the Obvious. A friend of mine cut the cost of renting a car in half by combining these two laws. Her travel plans were firm and established well in advance, and she was willing to commit herself to the car and the exact rental period weeks in advance. Carefully examining the car rental brochures, and questioning the rental agents, she learned that special rates could be applied for firm commitments made well in advance—just as with the airlines. Instead of signing up for a "reserve at anytime" rental, she found a way to trade a bit of flexibility (which she was not going to use) for substantial savings on the rental.

Try it. The next time you must make a hotel reservation, ask them for a special price in exchange for full payment a week or two in advance. Sure, there is risk involved, and if your plans are not firm you may not want to risk it. But if your travel plans are good and firm, take advantage of the savings. What you save will easily cover a Cancellation Insurance policy, with money to spare. Your risk with such a policy is reduced to virtually nothing.

Who writes such trip cancellation policies? The Travelers Insurance Companies of Hartford, Conn., does; so does Omaha Indemnity, a Mutual of Omaha company. Coverage of $1000 for one person might cost, say, under $40. They pay eligible expenses or reimburse you for nonrefundable trip expenses if you, a family member, traveling companion, or business partner falls ill, is injured, or dies, before or during your trip. Note that you can't cancel your trip just because you don't feel like going—the excuse must be injury, illness, or death. Look in the Yellow Pages under "Insurance Agents," note which ones offer trip cancellation insurance, and then call an agent for complete details.

Flexibility vs. Commitment

One of the criticisms leveled at our society is that people find it difficult to commit themselves for the long term. Whether it be a marriage, a mortgage, or a meal ticket, we're frightened of pinning ourselves down. In such a fluid society, how do we know that a better mate, or interest rate, or career is not just around the corner? And if it is, how can we grasp it if we're already committed? How can we give up our freedom to change our minds?

Finding the easier, or quicker, or less expensive way doesn't require genius. What's required is creativity, ingenuity, clear sight, and a willingness to explore new possibilities.

The more you do it, the easier you will find it. Usually our choices end up being ones of variety, not of quality—we end up buying a Ford rather than a Chevrolet, or flying on a Lockheed L-1011 rather than on a Boeing 747. Commitment means security, whereas freedom is by nature insecure.

PART ONE

How to Save
Money
Before
Leaving
Home

HOW TO SAVE MONEY
ON ALL YOUR TRAVELS

Saving money while traveling is never a simple matter—which is why, 19 years ago, the $15-a-Day Travel Club was formed. Actually, the idea came from readers of the Frommer/Pasmantier publications, who felt that such an organization could bring financial benefits, continuing travel information, and a sense of community to economy-minded travelers in all parts of the world. They were right.

In keeping with the money-saving concept, the membership fee is low, and it is immediately exceeded by the value of your benefits. Upon receipt of U.S. $12 (U.S. residents) or U.S. $15 (Canadian, Mexican, and other foreign residents) to cover one year's membership, we will send all new members by return mail (book rate):

(1) The latest edition of any *two* of the books listed on page 286.

(2) A copy of ARTHUR FROMMER'S GUIDE TO NEW YORK.

(3) A one-year subscription to the quarterly Club newspaper—THE WONDERFUL WORLD OF BUDGET TRAVEL (see below).

(4) Your personal membership card, which, once received, entitles you to purchase through the Club *all* Frommer/Pasmantier publications for a third to a half off their regular retail prices during the term of your membership.

These are the immediate and definite benefits which we can assure to members of the Club at this time. Even more exciting, however, are the further and more substantial benefits which it has been our continuing aim to achieve for members. These are announced in the Club's newspaper, *The Wonderful World of Budget Travel,* a full-size, eight-page newspaper that carries such continuing features as "Travelers' Directory"—a list of members all over the world who are willing to provide hospitality to other members as they pass through their home cities; "Share-a-Trip"—requests from members for travel companions who can share costs; "Readers Ask . . . Readers Reply"—travel-related queries from members, to which other members reply with firsthand information.

If you would like to join this hardy band of international budgeteers and participate in its exchange of information and hospitality, simply send U.S. $12 (U.S. residents) or $15 (Canadian, Mexican, and other foreign residents) along with your name and address to: $15-a-Day Travel Club, Inc., 1230 Avenue of Americas, New York, NY 10020. All foreign residents please pay by international postage money order in U.S. funds, or by a check drawn on a U.S. bank. Remember to specify which *two* of the books listed on page 286 you wish to receive in your initial package of members' benefits.

2

Why?, Where?, and When?—How to Select a Destination Wisely

If you answer the three questions above you will have begun preliminary planning for a successful, value-for-money trip. The questions will help you focus on *preparing yourself* for the trip, rather than preparing the trip itelf. Trips can't be prepared. Itineraries can be suggested, but bad flying weather, an unexpected festival (which causes you to stay longer), a romantic encounter, or a hot tip on a side trip will actually determine your true itinerary. Iron-clad itineraries result in the "It's Tuesday, this must be Belgium" syndrome.

Virtually no one has a clear picture of what traveling is, where they want to go, why they wish to go there, and what it's going to be like. Instead of a clear picture, our minds are cluttered with outdated information, stereotypes, prejudices, unfounded fears, flights of fancy, and simple ignorance. Without proper information, and a proper frame of mind, it's impossible to have an enjoyable trip; and an unpleasant or disappointing trip is the most expensive trip of all.

WHY ARE YOU GOING?

Keep your goal in mind. Why are you off on a trip? If the reason is just to get away from home, see new sights, meet new people, learn new things, then you're sure to succeed. "I've never been to Switzerland (or Arizona, or Tangier, or South America) and I just want to see what it's like." Bravo. But watch out for the hidden reason: "I'm an Anglophile and I'm lonely, so I'm going to England to meet the perfect mate." That may happen, but don't expect perfect mates to flock to the airport arrival gate. It's no easier to meet perfect mates on a trip than it is at home, and if you're confined to a ship, bus, or train for long periods and there's no one eligible aboard, it may be considerably harder. And did you expect England to be the land of your fairytales? All bowler hats and cozy pubs and Shakespeare? Don't be disappointed if it turns out to be a real country, with real people much like yourself, full of beauty and ugliness you never expected, and which never appeared in the fairytales.

Travel literature does little to help dispel stereotypes, simplifications, and false hopes. In fact, all travel brochures and most travel magazine articles and some guidebooks do all they can to encourage hazy visions of beauteous climes and cheery Munchkins: Rome without drizzle, Cairo without dust, Hollywood without smog. Did you know that Acapulco has more rainfall than any other place in Mexico? That weather in the Aegean is sometimes so bad that ferries to the Greek islands may not run for days? That visiting airy Phoenix can be bad for your asthma? All of these places are beautiful, and all are worth visiting, but they are real places with bad as well as good points. To know where you would like to go, you've got to have a clear idea of a place's true character—or at least throw out the stereotype—tell yourself "I *really* know *nothing* about New York (or Turkey, or Bolivia, or Quebec)" and suspend judgment until you arrive.

It's important that you keep your goal in mind so you can avoid disappointments; and avoiding disappointments—plus saving money—is the subject we take up next.

WHERE DO YOU REALLY WANT TO GO?

It may seem silly to bring up the question of destination. "I know where I'm going, thanks very much. My mind's made up."

But WHERE? is very closely associated with WHY? You've always wanted to see San Francisco or Switzerland, so you're going. Fine. Skip below to WHEN?

If you're still unsure about your destination, however, you have an even greater chance to save big money. An example: you live in the western part of North America, and you'd like to see some of the East. You could go to New York, Boston, or Montreal and have a wonderful time. But the price structure in these cities is quite high. Although inexpensive lodgings and meals are to be had, they're much more difficult to uncover. Substitute Halifax and a tour of Nova Scotia, instead of Boston and New England or Montreal and the Laurentians, and you'll have cut your expenses before even setting foot outside your front door. Or go to Portugal instead of France. Why did you want to go to France? To live in the midst of a storybook dream filled with boulevardiers, Hemingway and Fitzgerald, bistros and bonbons? If you were going to France to learn about French culture and to practice your French, then go, because you can't do that in less-expensive Portugal (though you *could* do it in less-expensive Quebec City). If, however, you just want to get away from home, dine on excellent food, experiment with some of the world's great wines, relax on sunny beaches, explore medieval fortresses and great museums, get to know an ancient and fascinating culture and its people, then go to Portugal and the savings over a comparable trip to France will astound you. On your next trip, head for Quebec, or fly off to a French-speaking Caribbean island in "shoulder" season or off-season, and you'll get your French practice at bargain rates.

Don't get me wrong. Paris is Paris, and when you truly want to go to Paris, nothing else will do. It all depends on WHY? you travel. Examine your travel objectives, choose your destination based on your true reasons for traveling (and an honest assessment of the destination), then move on to the all-important question of WHEN?

WHEN IS THE BEST TIME TO GO?

Everyone knows that there are "high" seasons and "low" seasons, and that one can save incredible amounts of money by visiting a country, city, or resort during the slack time. But this is not as easy as it sounds, for there are very good reasons why most people travel in high season. When it's freezing in Toronto, Hartford, and Seattle, that's the perfect time to head south to Mazatlan, Miami, and St. Thomas. We're back to the old question of WHY? you are traveling. To get away from the cold? Then you must go when it's cold up north and warm down south. Take off and enjoy it, follow the advice given later on in this book, and you'll still save money.

You might be surprised to learn, after asking yourself WHY?, that your true reason for heading to Florida is to take the kids to Disney World; that you're actually taking off to Mazatlan or Acapulco because it sounds exciting and foreign and the beaches are supposed to be so nice and the water so warm; or that you're headed for the Caribbean because for all these years you've wanted to see what these emerald islands looked like, rather than simply to get away from the cold.

Did you know that Acapulco has more rainfall than any other place in Mexico? That weather in the Aegean is sometimes so bad that ferries to the Greek islands may not run for days?

Go to Florida from late spring to late autumn, and you won't believe how cheap everything is: airfares, motels, special services such as deep-sea fishing or tours of the Everglades. The highways aren't crowded. Miami Beach is all yours. The seafood is cheaper. The same sort of inexpensive, leisurely, uncrowded travel is yours to be had in the Caribbean during this time.

With many destinations it's not so easy to determine the best, most cost-effective time to go. Austria would be lovely in August, yes? No. Sometimes it rains hard for days, particularly in August. The Greek islands are pretty far south, it must be like the Caribbean there in February? Wrong again. It's damp, and it drizzles, and many of the inexpensive small pensions have no heat, or are closed altogether. Quebec City would be a dull icebox in winter? Actually, Quebec's Winter Carnival is one of the most exciting, exhilarating, and enjoyable events of the year, well worth the trip. Forget Mexico in the summer, or Northern California in January? Not at all. You can go to Mexico City, or San Francisco, almost any time of year so far as the weather is concerned, because the climates of these two cities are equable year round.

How, then, does one choose a time to travel? By looking closely at information about climate, holidays and festivals, hotel prices and airfares. Every guidebook deals with the subject of when to go, and guidebooks are more trustworthy on this subject than are many materials produced by the local travel offices (which tend to want tourists to come even if the weather is terrible and all the museums are closed).

Ask friends who have been there. Study guidebooks, newspaper and magazine articles until you *have a sense* of what it will be like. Of course no friend, guidebook, or article can guarantee the weather. But with some research you can determine what your chances will be, and you can discover the climatic quirks of the area: rainy seasons and dry seasons, typhoon seasons and scirocco seasons, sunstroke seasons and black fly seasons.

Local Customs Affect Travel Plans and Costs

To get the most out of your trip for the least amount of money, you will have to study carefully more than just the weather at your destination. Look also at a calendar of holidays and festivals, and learn what importance they have. For instance, if you arrive in Israel on Friday evening, most everything will be locked up tight for the next 24 hours—it's the Sabbath.

You'll be able to get to your hotel (but only by taxi or shared taxi, not by bus); the hotel will be open (but not the bar, and perhaps not the restaurant); to go to a museum the next morning, you must have bought your ticket in advance, before the Sabbath began. It saves time, trouble, and money to arrive in Israel on a day other than Friday or Saturday.

A trip to France in the summer may sound great, but you can't try out all those little neighborhood restaurants (or many other attractions) in Paris in August, because virtually all of those little neighborhood restaurateurs—and their customers—have headed south for the traditional Parisian month on the Riviera.

Going to a Moslem country? The holy month of Ramadan, determined by the lunar calendar, comes at a slightly different time each year. In all Moslem countries—Morocco, Egypt, Turkey—daily life changes completely during the holy month. Business and museum schedules, restaurant hours, transportation timetables, all change to accommodate the daily fasting (from dawn to dusk) of the faithful. Want a cold Coke to lay the dust on a hot Cairo afternoon? Sorry. But come back at nightfall, and you can have all the Cokes you want—even dine on pigeons and figs until 4 or 5 o'clock in the morning.

Even less exotic destinations have quirks and foibles which can affect your travel plans—and costs—dramatically. In any French-speaking country, June 24th is a day to note. It's St. John the Baptist's Day (St-Jean Baptiste), and trains will be packed, inexpensive hotels jammed, and student eateries mobbed as young French, Belgian, and Swiss people take part in a midsummer frolic, the roots of which date back far beyond the beginning of Christianity. What it means for you is that you had better have a reserved seat on the train, a confirmed reservation in that inexpensive little Left Bank hotel, and the ability to deal with crowds. If not, you may find yourself paying a first-class fare for the only seat on the train, or staying in a fancy hotel at breathtaking prices.

A similar phenomenon closer to home is Columbus Day in New England. Virtually every room in every hotel, motel, inn, and guest house is booked in advance for this weekend, when the maple trees are usually in the full radiant blaze of their fall color.

If you just want to get away from home, dine on excellent food, experiment with some of the world's fine wines, relax on sunny beaches, explore medieval fortresses and museums . . . . then go to Portugal and the savings over a comparable trip to France will astound you.

But you get the idea. Anyone can tell you a time—perhaps only a day or two—when a local event changes daily life drastically and makes things difficult, or more expensive, for the casual traveler. These events may have little to do with the weather, or the normal tourist season, or any other predictable aspect. You've got to find out about such phenomena before you plan your trip. In finding out, you'll learn a tremendous amount about the place and the culture you're about to explore. In short, you'll be prepared to take full advantage of your travel opportunity.

Weight + Weather = Money

Another aspect of WHEN? is packing, and in this respect weather equals money. You simply cannot travel heavy and travel cheaply at the same time. You must travel as lightly as possible so you can walk the several blocks from the terminal to your hotel rather than taking a cab; so that you won't need to tip porters, or pay for luggage lockers; so that you won't waste time dealing with *things* when you should be out on the beach, or in a museum, or trying the local delicacies. And the weight of your bags is directly related to the weather. Go to Rome in the summer, and all you'll need is a few drip-dry things, sandals, and a sun hat (when you wash your clothes, they'll dry in minutes in the arid Roman air). But go to Rome in the winter and you'll need a sweater, a raincoat, perhaps an umbrella and rubber boots. Go to Newport, Rhode Island, in the summer for the America's Cup races and you'd better have a few sharp sporting outfits and some formal clothes, or you won't be able to try many of the best restaurants. Dress codes are strict in Newport, especially in summer. There's more to come on the subject of packing, but for now, keep in mind that "weight plus weather equals money."

3

Information Pays—and Much of It Is Free

Time is money, weather is money, but most of all *information is money*. This is true in every aspect of life, but doubly important if you want to get the most out of your travel dollar. A Harvard education, thirty years' experience, the "inside story," a hot tip—all these are types of information, and all are obviously worth money. In travel, information is crucial and immediately useful, because if you've never heard about that cheap charter flight, you will certainly end up paying the higher scheduled airline fare, and if you don't know that Mrs. Smith operates a guest house on Main Street you will end up checking into the Holiday Inn out on the highway. Most of the information you will need on your trip—no matter where you're going—is available to you right now, very cheaply, at home. The rest is available near your destination, and it, too, is mostly free, or very inexpensive.

You must take the time to get information and then you must take the time to absorb it. As we've seen, knowing in detail about weather, and high and low seasons, and local holidays, can affect your travel budget directly and immediately. But you've got to learn about these things *before you go*. Don't pick up a guidebook on the way to the airport, planning to read it on the plane. By then it may be too late to take advantage of the information the guidebook provides. When you get to your destination, you may spend several dollars for a local map when you could have had a much better map *completely free* by writing to the local tourist office in advance of your departure. (When you get to where you're going, the free maps may not be available. Local map vendors may put pressure on the tourist office not to give maps away; besides, the tourist office would rather send you a map, thereby helping to convince you to come, than provide you with a free map once you're there.)

Start planning for your trip early. Choose your guidebook; send away for information, maps, schedules, and brochures; meet with friends who have been there; and visit several travel agents. Do all this months before you leave.

If you plan to travel with others, especially children, one of the smartest things you can do is to involve them in the information-gathering process very early. This takes some of the burden off you, and builds their enthusiasm as well. For more on this idea, see Chapter 15—The Special Traveler, under "Family Travel."

SOURCES OF FREE INFORMATION

Virtually every city, state, and country wants to encourage tourism. Tourists bring money and they take back memories that are a valuable public relations resource for the city, state or country concerned.

Every tourist destination—down to tiny villages in remote places—generates tourism information, mostly in printed form, but sometimes also in the form of a person (more or less knowledgeable) who staffs a booth or a desk and provides guidance to visitors in person or by phone. Virtually all of this information is free, though for a few items you may have to pay a nominal charge to cover printing costs.

> Time is money, weather is money, but
> most of all, information is money.

Tourism jurisdictions usually overlap. For instance, if you're planning a trip to Montreal, you could get lots of information from the Canadian Government Office of Tourism, which has offices throughout the United States and Canada. Also, the Province of Quebec would be glad to provide you with lists of accommodations, parks, activities, and special events. The City of Montreal would happily send you a detailed street plan, a plan of the fabulous Metro system, a list of good restaurants, a guide to museums (with hours of operation, telephone numbers, etc.), and perhaps a few discount coupons to this or that. You can even delve deeper. Every hotel will gladly send you a brochure, and a price list, plus news on any special deals currently available. Many restaurants have reduced-format sample menus which they'd love to tempt you with. The museums will send brochures, notices of special exhibits, floorplans. In fact, the quantity of information that's yours for the asking is so great, you'll have the delightful problem of *too much* information, rather than not enough.

How do you get all this? Often, you don't even need the proper address. If you know the right city, just make up an address if you can't find the right one easily. Something like "Tourism Information Office,

Department of Commerce, Commonwealth of Pennsylvania, Harrisburg, PA" will no doubt get you whatever you want: a good Pennsylvania map, list of state parks and camping areas, details on hunting season, on local vineyards (there are lots!), walking tours of Philadelphia. If you don't get the information itself, you'll at the very least obtain the exact address from which the information may be had.

Foreign addresses are no problem. "Ministry of Tourism, Ankara, Turkey," may result in a slim envelope with exotic stamps, or a thick information-crammed envelope from the Ministry of Tourism office in New York. You could have written to New York in the first place, had you known. But if you didn't, no matter. Given time, some official in Ankara will translate your request and see that it's passed on for action.

Be aware that the quality and amount of information available from tourist offices will vary. For example, Canada and Britain both provide first-rate and abundant information, as do New York state and Tennessee. Other countries and regions may not supply as much or as detailed information as they do, but it will still be helpful.

As I said at the beginning of this chapter, information pays. To help you in your search for information we've listed the addresses of tourist offices of countries and regions throughout the world and the 50 states of the United States. See Appendix 1, page 252.

What to Expect from a Tourist Office

What can you get if you send a card to a city, state, or national tourist office? That depends upon the particular tourist office: some are astoundingly efficient and well prepared; others are woeful holes for petty bureaucrats, somebody's relatives, and time-servers. If you have specific desires, always *ask*: request the basics specifically, and *give a deadline* by which the information must reach you. Here are the basics:

MAPS: Quality and detail may vary, but every office hands out maps. Ask for a country map and city maps as you need them. If you want special interest maps—nautical maps of the Maine coast, hiking routes in Nepal, railroad lines in Switzerland—ask where you can get them.

HOTEL INFORMATION: You may get a short list of names with telephone numbers and official class rankings (Luxury, First Class, etc.), which is next to useless; or you may get a thick book with everything you could want. Prince Edward Island puts out a provincial lodgings guide which gives a description of every single lodging place on the island, with its exact location, mail address and phone number, prices, number and type of rooms (cabins, housekeeping, etc.), other facilities (swimming pool or whatever), and tips on reservations or what to do nearby. This book is free. Nova Scotia's is almost as good, and it, too, is free. Both guides also include lists of campgrounds.

The British Tourist Authority also provides exemplary materials. Write to them, and you can get a "Map and List of 100 Inexpensive Hotels," or a directory of sumptuous castles and manor houses that have been converted into hotels, or a list of homey bed-and-breakfast lodgings in Stratford-upon-Avon.

The only problem with such hotel information is that it is impartial. Choosing a hotel is one situation in which partiality is a virtue. Whereas a travel writer, in an article or guidebook, will advise you that some hotels are overpriced and others offer great value-for-money, an official information source will stick to bare statistics and will not—indeed is forbidden to—offer an opinion about a hotel's relative value.

RESTAURANT INFORMATION: It is much less common to receive detailed restaurant data, and restaurant recommendations made by official people suffer from the same weakness as official hotel data: impartiality. Of two restaurants which meet the same official criteria for three stars (or three forks, or whatever), one may be rather scruffy and one may be superb, though both charge the same prices. Again, a travel or dining guide is of much more value, providing that it's opinionated and exclusive (i.e., it puts some restaurants in and leaves others out).

DATA ON WHAT TO SEE AND DO: You'll receive lots and lots of this, and most of it will be excellent. Booklets which outline walking tours—with maps—are a common item. Auto itineraries are also popular. Read them carefully before you set out, because impartiality comes into play here, too. The tourist office wants to spread out the tourist dollars as evenly as possible, so they'll map out routes into the boonies where there is little of real interest to see or do—they want to get you out of the major attraction centers (where you'll probably go anyway) into the backlands which could use some infusions of cash.

OTHER INFORMATION: The miscellaneous information you will receive may be the most important: weather data and temperature charts, lists of festivals and holidays, train and bus schedules, cruise ship itineraries.

Other Sources of Free Information

Use your library. Once you've decided on your destination, read as much as you possibly can about the country, city, or resort. At the local library consult the *Readers' Guide to Periodical Literature* for a listing of the latest articles that have been published by magazines like *Travel/Holiday, Gourmet,* and *Sunset* about your destination.

Another good source of almost-free information is the State Department, which publishes backgrounds on particular countries throughout the world. Write to the Superintendent of Documents, U. S. Government Printing Office, Washington, DC 20402 (tel. 202/783-3238), for a list of available backgrounds. The department publishes one background per month containing useful information about a specific country's government, people, climate, and health hazards. Each one costs 50¢.

About the best all-around source of travel information is the same it has been for centuries past: other travelers.

And don't forget the newspapers. Admittedly the travel sections of the smaller newspapers may not be too useful, but at your library you should be able to find your closest large metro daily or the *New York Times,* the *Los Angeles Times,* the *Washington Post,* or the *New York Daily News,* all of which carry excellent Sunday travel sections.

TRAVEL AGENTS—WHAT THEY DO FOR FREE

A good travel agent can be a valuable source of information. The best agents are professionals who take pride in keeping abreast of all the fast-breaking developments in the frenetic travel industry. They'll gladly give you tips on the most cost-effective transportation and lodgings, visa requirements, currency regulations, and travel advisories. (The U.S. Department of State issues travel advisories for countries and areas where unrest may threaten tourism, and your travel agent should be on their mailing list.) Travel agents get commissions from hotels and transportation lines for each booking. Thus, there's a built-in incentive to book you on the most expensive flight and into the most expensive hotel room. But good agents know that this will ultimately lose them customers, so they depend on volume and customer confidence to provide enough bookings to pay the rent.

Bad travel agents are easy to find. It's tempting to be lazy, or to open an office just to take advantage of the "fam trips" (familiarization tours) to exotic places, or just for the discounts on flights and rooms which travel agents receive, or even to take advantage of the tax benefits. Still, such travel agents are few; most travel agents perform invaluable services. How, then, do you find a good one?

How to Find a Good Travel Agent

The best course, until you've discovered an agent in whom you can put all your trust, is to make appointments at two or even three agencies and propose exactly the same trip to each. See what each comes up with, then compare results. Make your visits within a few days, for schedules, fares, and seat availability can change overnight, and it's not fair to blame an agency for a cancellation or fare hike which is out of its control. When you propose your trip, remember that you don't have to buy, or even book, reservations right then. The agent may urge you to do so—with all the data right there on the computer screen, it's simple to type the booking in. If the agent says, "The flight is almost full," or "The hotel's just about booked up," answer that you'll give your decision within 24 hours. (As you check at the next agency, you may well find that the plane has lots of empty seats!)

You might also check to make sure that your target agents are members of the American Society of Travel Agents, 711 Fifth Avenue, New York, NY 10022 (tel. 212/486-0700). Also, check whether your local Better Business Bureau has any record of complaints against them. (If you ever wish to lodge a complaint against a travel agent you can write to the consumer affairs department of the ASTA and your local Better Business Bureau.)

Don't underestimate the helpfulness of a good travel agent. You pay no more for their services; you pay no less if you do their work yourself. An example of this helpfulness: when you fly to Mexico, an agent should obtain the required Mexican Tourist Card for you along with your air ticket. You give the agent your passport number, or a copy of your birth certificate or voter registration card, and the work is all done before you even get to the airport.

THE MOST ACCURATE FREE INFORMATION OF ALL

About the best all-around source of travel information is the same as it's been for centuries past: *other travelers*. Everyone wants to talk about a recent trip or travel experience. You can approach a total stranger, ask about a certain route, city, or difficult border crossing, and you'll get the stranger's total life story, for free. The trick is not to depend on any one bit of information. Ask numerous other travelers until you have confirmed the data you first received.

Don't leave this source of information unexploited; don't leave meetings with other travelers to chance.

Seek out people with fresh experience of the place: ask travel agents, and friends, and local cultural societies to put you in touch with someone who has recently returned. Remember, everyone wants to talk about a trip. You're doing a favor (to them and to yourself) by listening.

USE YOUR TELEPHONE!

In the realm of low-cost information, the telephone is tops. At the end of the month, when your phone bill comes, you're going to think this advice doesn't make sense: "I spent $15, just on calls to find out details of this trip!" But look at it this way. Just about every other source of information—guidebooks, free travel folders, advice from friends, even queries by mail—is one-way (they give you data, and you pick out what you want), or more or less out of date, or both. With the telephone, you can go instantly to the prime source of the information, and you can pump that source of information in detail; furthermore, you can request action. "Send me some brochures," "Make my reservation," "Let me know when the date is set," and *you can hold someone responsible*: "I spoke with Mr. Quiensabé on March third, and he said the price was $39"; "Mrs. Noncomprendo, of your office, told me the festival had been cancelled".

Obviously, you don't want to use the phone when there is a cheaper way of obtaining the information; one wouldn't call London to ask about the *QE2*'s cruise schedule when any local travel agent would have it. But you can call the U.S. Department of State's Citizens' Emergency Center (tel. 202/632-5225) and ask if there has been a Travel Advisory issued for this or that country, and get an official opinion on the safety and comfort, and advisability, of travel to any disturbed area. No more fretting over ominous newspaper and radio reports: you'll *know*. Or you can call that little hotel in Paris, tell them you've heard rumors that everything there is booked solid for next week, and ask if they have a room: "How much? Is that the only one? Is there anything else nearby that you know of? Would you tell them I'll mail a deposit? What's the weather like? How many francs to the dollar these days? My name is Tom, I'll see you in a week."

You must take the time to get the
information and to absorb it. . . . Knowing
in detail about weather, high and low
seasons, and local holidays can directly
affect your travel budget.

All this would cost $4.13. To call London is even cheaper. The alternative is to fret, and worry, and send letters (at 40¢ a shot), and arrive after a long flight in Paris with no information on the room situation and less than 12 hours in which to locate one in your price range. Once you're on the ground, you can take care of everything locally. But for planning, nothing beats the telephone.

Please, please note that I recommend using the telephone this way only when calling from the United States and Canada. In most of the world, telephone charges are still absurdly high for long-distance or international calls. A three-minute call from Detroit to Athens might cost $4.13; the same call dialed from Athens to Detroit might cost $40 or more.

4

Choosing a Guidebook

Travel guidebooks spring to mind as the prime source of low-cost travel information. Data that has cost thousands and thousands of dollars to collect, compose, and disseminate is yours for a very small number of dollars. If you refer to a guidebook a half-dozen times, you've already got your money's worth from it in terms of utility. Dollar for dollar, any good guidebook is ridiculously cheap, no matter what the cover price.

Still, we're concerned here with getting the very most from every dollar spent for travel-related items, so let's examine now the ways to get the best guidebook for the money.

HOW GUIDEBOOKS ARE MADE

Guidebooks have been around for a very long time. Centuries ago, travelers returning from exotic lands would write their memoirs or edit their travel diaries and publish the results. These travelogues were useful to the next traveler, as well as entertaining to "armchair travelers."

Today, many of the best guidebooks are made the same way: an observant traveler who is also a good writer goes out in search of fulfilling travel experiences, and describes them in detail for his or her readers. In an age of big organizations and bureaucracies, it's refreshing to know that some people are still doing their jobs the good old way: hitting the road with notebook in hand to observe in person, and to pass on important information to those who will come after.

Alas, this sort of one-author guidebook is becoming scarce as the world gets more hectic, more complicated, and more expensive. Other ways of collecting data have been created, and these ways have advantages and disadvantages.

Books written by committee are often found on bookstore shelves. Instead of one travel writer, a number of writers collaborate to prepare a guide to a large area. Each may take a geographic area, in which case the book will have the character of a mini-collection of one-author books. What the book may lack is the unifying overview which a single author can give: a restaurant in Los Angeles can't truly be judged "as good as" a restaurant in New York, because different people have investigated them.

Some guides attempt to solve this problem by having a single set of criteria—a common checklist against which any establishment or travel experience can be measured. Hotels are ranked, and awarded "stars," on the basis of such things as number of elevators, restaurant seating capacity, multilingual staff, or elaborateness of plumbing. Unfortunately, there is little room in such listings for intangibles: ambience, convenience, friendliness, security, propriety, which a single travel writer would have taken into account in a recommendation.

A single travel writer, a committee of travel writers, an army of checklist-bearing data-collectors—there is yet another way guidebooks are put together. This method might be called "stringers and editors." "Stringers," part-time help who live in tourist destinations, send data to an editor in a central office, and the editor puts it together in a book. Many books are written by this method; the advantages are obvious: no big travel expenses sending a writer to the destination, perhaps to stay for months; fresh data from stringers who know the territory because they live there; lower overhead through utilization of part-time help (the stringers) and only one full-time person (the editor).

Dollar for dollar, any good guidebook is ridiculously cheap, no matter what the cover price.

The disadvantages of "stringers and editors" are not quite so apparent, but are extremely important. First, the stringers are not tourists; they live there, and they may find it difficult to see the place through a tourist's eyes. In their daily lives, they may not encounter the many puzzling situations in which a stranger would find him or herself. Also, for stringers the data collection is only a part-time job, which they may or may not think to be important. The editor will probably never know if a stringer sends in data of mediocre quality. The editor may never have been to the place in question, and may inadvertently produce useless recommendations. For instance, the advice to "call for reservations" at a busy restaurant may be useless in a Third World city where the telephones hardly ever work; or, "the taxi fare is $3" will do you little good in a resort with a notorious shortage of cabs. The information given is not wrong, it's just useless. Why pay for it? A travel writer on-the-spot would have recommended that you drop by the restaurant the day before to make your reservation, that you take a bus (or reserve your taxi in advance) in that cab-short resort.

In their quest for lower expenses and higher profits, some publishing companies have pushed credibility to the limit. You can pay good money these days for guidebooks which are mostly "boilerplate," rambling prose touching on this or that aspect of the destination involved, more or less entertaining stuff, but hardly what you'd call useful or significant. Boilerplate rarely goes out of date. Some background information is helpful, but too much is a cost-cutting caper, a way of selling cheap goods expensively.

Other ways in which some publishers lower expenses and raise profits: they don't pay stringers at all, just an editor who garners information of dubious freshness and importance from other published materials—mostly the free tourist-office stuff you can send away for—adds a few maps and some filler copy, and sells the resultant book at a premium price. You don't know you've bought a useless commodity until you are well along in your trip, and by then it's too late.

Payoffs

Cynics believe that most travel writers are on the take, benefiting from free hotel rooms, free transportation, free meals, all in exchange for good recommendations in their writings. In fact, this practice is relatively rare. Governments will often provide some help with the expensive initial edition of a guidebook: they may arrange for reduced airfares or hotel rooms, and may arrange to purchase a certain number of copies of the guide, just to assure that a new guide to their territory comes into existence. But actual quid pro quo's are rare. Newspapers often skirt close to the line by featuring travel articles on places that buy large ads in the travel section. But I've never heard of editors actually taking kickbacks, and any good newspaper travel editor will put the overall interest and balance of the section above mere gross advertising revenue.

In one case, a series of lodging guides collects a payoff by suggesting that establishments listed in the guides would want to join a small association ostensibly set up to maintain lodging standards. The dues are high. In fact, then, the hotels and inns which join the association are paying for their advertisements to appear in the books. This would be fine, except that the reader thinks he's getting an unbiased recommendation for the establishment in question, which is not the case—it's a paid advertisement instead.

HOW TO CHOOSE A GUIDEBOOK

With all these caveats, and a number of dubious practices, how does the beleaguered traveler choose the best guidebook? It's not impossible. Here's what to do.

Know Your Needs

First toss out the notion that there is such a thing as "the best guidebook." Guides are written to appeal to specific segments of the traveling public, so the first thing you must do is to locate those guides that fit your trip. Are you going on a two-week charter vacation, with your transportation and accommodations already arranged and paid for? Then look for a series of pocket guides that have details on sightseeing, activities, and the local cuisine. Are you off on a two-month, low-budget vagabond tour? The guide for you is the one chock full of budget travel tips, inexpensive lodging recommendations, and directions to cheap eateries.

Check the Copyright Date

Now that you have narrowed the field down to the guides which fit your trip, turn to the back of the title page and look for the copyright date. Ignore the dates on the cover. By law, the copyright date is supposed to be that of the year of publication, or up to one month earlier (that is, a book published in December 1982 can bear the words "Copyright © 1983"). In recent years, however, some guidebook publishers have ignored the law, and have published guides in late summer and early autumn with *next year's* copyright dates. This is unfair, but it should reinforce in your mind the thought that *any guidebook is at least nine months old by the time you buy it*. It may be several years old; it is prohibitively expensive to re-collect, re-edit, reprint and distribute books every few months, and so the book will be on sale for at least a year after it appears, perhaps more.

Is this a rip-off? Not at all. You could have fresh data every three months, but you'd have to be willing to pay hundreds of dollars for it rather than $6 to $10. All guidebooks suffer from this time lag. Your job is to choose the one which gives you the freshest and most plenteous data for your particular kind of trip, all for the lowest price.

Look for Detailed Factual Information

Now it's time to look inside. How much "boiler-plate" is there? A hundred, two hundred pages of background filler? Do you want it? You'll have to pay for it, and then you'll have to carry it!

What about the highly perishable information: prices, timetables, individual recommendations for lodgings and restaurants. There are none, or very few? This perishable information is the most difficult and expensive to keep up to date, and if a guide has little of it, the book's price had better be low. It's fine to blather on in glowing tones about a charming restaurant or cozy country inn, but if the guide gives you no idea of the cost, what good is it? Actual prices, rather than headings such as "Inexpensive" or "Moderate," are the best, even if inflation has by now left them behind (as it usually has). One quickly learns to compensate by raising the price a certain percentage. But if the charming elderly couple who run that lovely inn are already charging $90 a night, you probably know what you need to know. Maybe the price is $105 now, maybe it's not. It's out of range.

In recommending an establishment, does the guide tell you where it is, with driving or walking directions rather than just a mailing address? If there's a paragraph raving about a good restaurant on Ibn Gevirol Street in Tel Aviv, does it give more than the street number? Ibn Gevirol Street is miles and miles long! What about hours of operation, telephone numbers, post office box numbers? It's difficult to say how much of this detailed information you will actually need. But if it's not there in the first place, it certainly won't be there when you need it. You can always find out such little facts somewhere else, but then why pay a guidebook publishing company for work you'll end up doing yourself? Guidebooks should *guide,* telling you just about everything you would want—or, more important, *need*—to know.

Too Many Lists?

Look closely at the book's organization. Are there bare lists of places, or outline-type categorical lists with essential data? These are signs of the clipboard mentality, and out on the road they are very hard to use. A list of every modern hotel in town, with phone number, minimum double room price, and symbols denoting the various facilities? How will you tell the difference from one to the other, except for price and whether or not it has a swimming pool? And those little symbols will drive you crazy! Is there an entire paragraph or page listing all the golf courses, or tennis courts, or museums in the city or country? With a bare list, how will you ever find out which bus to take, or when they're open, or what they charge, or what makes them worthwhile? Remember, editors *love* lists like this: they're simple to compile at a desk miles from the travel scene, they make logical sense, they look impressive—but in fact they're very difficult for the traveler on the spot to use, or even worse, they're entirely useless.

What about finding things quickly? Does the book's structure make sense to you? After a minute or two, can you turn to the information you desire quickly, without much trouble? The book's structure should fit the traveler's actual, practical, on-the-spot needs, and not some editorial requirement or mechanistic system.

And Finally, Read!

Now for the final acid test: *read*. Pick a spot that interests you, something that deals with actual situations you will encounter in daily life—visiting a sight, having a meal, finding a hotel, booking transportation. It should seem as though you're asking a trusted friend, who's been there, to explain what it's actually like. Soon you will come across the telltale hints and suggestions that let you know the writer has been there and has been through it: "When touring in Burma I strongly advise that you wear sandals rather than shoes—simply because you take them off and put them on so often when visiting temples and pagodas." (Tony Wheeler, in *Burma—a travel survival kit*, Lonely Planet, 1979). No editor sitting at a desk, no stringer who had last visited the temples and pagodas years ago, would have thought to suggest such a practical matter. Things that are giveaways to a bad book: lack of prices, phone numbers, and *directions*. I was astounded to read in one guidebook a description of a lovely park, excellent for a picnic, "on the outskirts of Mexico City"! Hundreds of square miles of urban sprawl, millions and millions of people, and the only direction to this lovely park is that it is "on the outskirts"? How much priceless travel time will you have to spend to find it? How much is such a recommendation worth?

Some background information is helpful, but too much is a cost-cutting caper, a way of selling cheap goods expensively.

It is not just the burgeoning complexity of the world that has made such detailed information crucial. Indeed, it is more important now than ever before to have exact, complete, up-to-date data. But good guidebooks have always given detailed information and hints drawn from on-the-spot observation. In 1907 the venerable Karl Baedeker was advising travelers, in his *Handbook for Travellers: SWITZERLAND* (22nd edition), that "at the second-class inns the average charges are: bedroom 1½–2 francs, breakfast 1–1¼ francs, table d'hôte 2–3 francs, service discretionary, and no charge for 'bougies' " (candles). And another helpful tip: "If a prolonged stay is made at a hotel the bill should be asked for every three or four days, in order that errors, whether accidental or designed, may more easily be detected."

Guidebooks by Frommer/Pasmantier

You might think that I, as a writer of Frommer/Pasmantier guidebooks, must be prejudiced in favor of our company's books. That's true, I am—and here's why:

Frommer/Pasmantier has purposely kept a small, informal structure. Our office in New York's Simon and Schuster Building is a congenial place where a small crew of travel-mad people edit manuscripts, read letters from travelers who have used our guides, and keep abreast of fast-breaking developments in the travel industry. Each guidebook is the responsibility of a single author or a two-author team (though the massive *Dollarwi$e Guide to Canada* has a three-author team), not a sprawling network of contributors or a huge committee of clipboard-carrying data collectors. Our efforts are personal, our contacts are personal, and our approach to travel writing is personal. The guides are filled with the worldly-wise opinions of our writers, who are beholden to no airline or hotel chain, no restaurant or national tourism ministry.

Our books are filled with precise, on-the-spot descriptions of hotels, restaurants, and tourist facilities, with exact prices, timetables, telephone numbers, addresses, and enough background to convey the "mood" of each establishment.

In the years I have worked for Frommer/Pasmantier, I've gotten to know thousands of our readers. Many a "letter to the author" has resulted in a lively correspondence which is informative for both parties. From this experience, I have learned that our readers are of all ages, but always young-at-heart and ready for adventure. Most have money to spend, but are very careful to get value-for-money when they spend it. Many are experienced travelers and repeat buyers of our books, and quite a few buy successive editions of a particular guide for successive trips to the same destination. These readers tend to look upon a current guidebook as a cost-effective information resource, not as a guide through perilous unknown waters.

It is extremely important to us to give our readers a value-for-money product, because our success depends upon it. We are not an auto club that charges annual dues, we do not accept advertisements, we do not sell stickers or signs that say "Recommended in Our Guidebook." We exist because masses of readers find our guides to be of value—and our readership is the most demanding and aware.

This is not to say that Frommer/Pasmantier guidebooks are the only ones that will fit your needs. There are many excellent guides on the market. But there are many, many others which are of dubious value: it is simple to fill a book up with words, but quite another thing to create a book which truly *guides*. A true guide must anticipate questions and problems, and then stand ready to solve them with the right information in the right place. A true guide is beholden only to its readers, for they are the ones who keep it alive.

At the Cash Register

Once you've narrowed your choice down to one or two guidebooks, look at the prices. Price is important only in relation to what's inside the book. The book looks great, and it costs only $7? That's an incredible bargain! If it looks great and it costs $12, or even $15 or $20, it's probably still a bargain. If you've found the precise book that fits your needs, buy it regardless of price. When you're about to spend hundreds or thousands of dollars on a trip, don't quibble about a few dollars. The right guidebook can almost make or break your trip.

If your choice comes down to several books, buy by price, or by sturdiness, or by weight and size, or by whether or not the book includes photographs. Don't buy more than you need, don't buy less than you need. Buy what fits.

5

Reap Rewards by Advance Planning

Good strategic planning is the first requirement for a successful cost-effective trip. Failing to plan well is like forgetting your suitcase: you've got to get everything together on the road, in unfamiliar territory, perhaps at higher-than-home prices.

BEFORE YOU GO

You've sent away for free information and maps, you've chosen the right guidebook, you've checked out the weather and the holiday calendar for your destination. Now you're ready to tackle the specifics of preparation. Read the following detailed alphabetical checklist carefully, because you can recoup the few dollars you spent on this book by taking advantage of just a few of the suggestions given.

Cameras and Film

I have not heard of any country where film and photographic supplies are cheaper than in the U.S. Kodak is the world leader, and though foreign films may be cheaper than Kodak in a film store abroad, nothing will be cheaper than film bought in the U.S. Buy what you think you'll need. If you have extra, sell it abroad, or bring it home, store it in the refrigerator, and use it later. The price of film only goes up.

Kodak has processing plants in various parts of the world. Good processing is available (but expensive) in the developed countries. Be very careful about processing in developing countries. If you must get film developed in the Third World, get a recommendation from a consulate, local professional photographer, or newspaperman, somebody who *knows*. Don't just ask a photo shopkeeper if he does good work.

As for equipment, it, too, can be more expensive, even in the country of its origin. Prices these days have less to do with costs of production than with taxes, duties, and market factors. Before you rush off to Japan or Germany or Switzerland to buy camera gear, have current information on prices.

The same goes for duty-free shops, many of which save you very little. (See Chapter 13 for details.)

Discount Deals

Perhaps the best money-saving reason for doing your planning well in advance is so that you can take advantage of the many discount deals available only to those who think ahead. Special discounts on airline fares are often applied if you buy your ticket several weeks in advance; the cheapest seats on every plane are very limited in number—the airlines put them there mostly so they can advertise the low fares—and you want to be one of the few lucky people who gets such a seat. (See Chapter 7.)

Discounts are also available for other modes of transportation—investigate railroad passes like the Eurailpass, BritRail Pass, or the Amtrak equivalent (when it's offered); and bus passes like those offering unlimited travel on Trailways or Greyhound for one, two, or three weeks at a special low price. Similar deals are offered throughout the world, and if you ask about transportation deals when you write for tourist information or make your travel reservations, you can find out what's current.

Perhaps the best money-saving reason for doing your planning well in advance is so that you can take advantage of the many discount deals available only to those who think ahead.

Transportation is not the only field for organized discounts. Lodging discount plans are becoming very popular, especially in Europe off-season. National tourist offices, airlines, regional associations, or hotel chains may offer coupons good for a night's lodging at participating hotels, and these coupons will be priced far below the normal room price. Why do they do it? What's the catch? Won't they lose money? The answer is that the region has excess hotel capacity off-season, and a room unsold for a night is a room that costs money to maintain but has produced no income. So, if they require you to buy five or ten coupons, they'll have guaranteed some income for five or ten days for the room. Finland has such a plan: pay $24 per check for a book of four "Finncheques," and you get a night's accommodation for each check in any of 138 hotels in 66 cities and towns. Want to go deluxe?

Pay another $10 per check and you've got first-class or luxury accommodations.

One such incredible lodging offer was recently advertised by British Airways: for standby passengers flying in winter, rooms in central London were sold at $20 single, $30 double, tax, service, and continental breakfast included! These rooms were in various Grand Metropolitan hotels; they were priced at $140 in high season. See Chapter 10 for more tips on similar bargains. The point to be made here is that you must know about such things *in advance*.

Besides transportation and accommodation, sightseeing and nightlife are often heavily discounted. The Netherlands National Tourist Office, 576 Fifth Avenue, New York, NY 10036 (tel. 212/245-4320), will sell you a "Holland Culture Card" for $5. With the card, you get free entry to 170 museums and landmarks, special deals on concert and ballet tickets, even a discount on rail travel. But you have to order the card before you leave home.

The Danish Tourist Board, 75 Rockefeller Plaza, New York, NY 10019 (tel. 212/582-2802), and Scandinavian Airlines System will sell you a special book of coupons good for discounts on meals, cover charges at nightclubs, museums, and even a hydrofoil ride to Sweden. The coupons are all for use in Copenhagen, off-season.

All these discounts are normal examples of what is available. The gimmicks change with the seasons, and a special deal for last winter may not be offered next winter—you've got to do some research to find what is current, and then you must order in advance.

KEEPING UP-TO-DATE: Obviously, the way to keep track of all the latest promotions offered by airlines, car rental companies, tour packagers, etc., is to scan the major travel magazines and newspapers for advertisements. Or you can subscribe to one of the recent crop of travel newsletters. Two of the most useful are:

The Joy of Travel (formerly *Joyer Travel Report*), Phillips Publishing Inc., 7315 Wisconsin Ave., Bethesda, MD 20814 (tel. 301/ 986-0666), monthly, $60 a year.

Travel Smart, Communications House, 40 Beechdale Rd., Dobbs Ferry, NY 10522 (tel. 914/693-8300), monthly, $26 a year.

Before subscribing to any newsletter, write and request a sample copy.

Electrical Appliances, Adapters, Plugs

You shouldn't be carrying too much of this stuff around with you. It's heavy and it causes problems. After having two transformers melted down by power surges in developing countries, I no longer take my electric razor. I take a safety razor and brushless shaving cream.

Hair dryers are also a problem. They may sell you one with "European adapters," and 220-volt current capability, but it may not do all it is supposed to do. For Europe, one needs at least three and perhaps four different plugs to cover all bases. Consider alternative methods of drying your hair: lamps, the sun, a borrowed hair dryer, a heating duct. If you must have your own dryer, get a small one. Current in Canada, the U.S., Mexico, and most of Central America is 120 volts, 50 or 60 cycles, with the flat-prong American-style plugs. In the rest of the world, current is usually 220–240 volts, 50 or 60 cycles, and the plugs can be anything from the monster three-prong-and-pound-of-plastic British "safety plug" to the flimsy Italian two-round-prong ones. Try to find out what you'll need for the country you're visiting. Don't worry about it too much. If you don't have the proper plug or adapter, drop in at any little electric supply shop at your destination and they'll probably have what you need.

Insurance (Against Theft and Loss)

Before you assume that your standard homeowner's insurance policy will cover any losses outside the home, check with your insurance agent. Often you must pay an additional sum for outside insurance; also the policy may stipulate coverage limits on certain objects: jewelry, cash, and furs, for instance.

Even if your own home policy will cover losses while you're traveling you may still want to take out a baggage insurance policy, because (1) the deductible will be less (often as low as $25), and (2) you may not want to claim against your homeowner's policy and thus increase future premiums. Furthermore, a homeowner's policy does not always cover the loss (as against theft) of your baggage. A baggage policy will, although it will probably exclude such items as money, tickets, documents, etc. The cost of such a policy is based on how long you'll be away and how much coverage you want. Remember—you'll need evidence of any loss or theft to make a claim on the insurance policy.

Medical Matters

Travelers in Europe, the United States and Canada, Australia, New Zealand, and Japan need not worry much about vaccinations and inoculations against disease. But in the rest of the world, generally speaking, you had better look into the matter closely. Malaria, for instance, is on the *increase*—contrary to the popular belief that disease is everywhere being beaten back. Cholera, too, is rearing its ugly head, and it's spread throughout the world by people traveling in jet planes. In some cases, as with malaria, it's right to fear the disease itself; in others, like cholera, you can be pretty sure of not contracting the illness if you take simple hygienic precautions—but border officials may not let you cross from a cholera area if you haven't had an inoculation. No matter how you swear you're free of the disease, they'll ask for documented proof. You may spend a week waiting in line at a clinic of questionable sanitation, with everyone else in town, to get the shot. When cholera breaks out, pandemonium does too. Few people die, some get sick, many are inconvenienced. You want to be none of the above.

One way to minimize the risk of illness is to know the health hazards to expect, get as much information as you possibly can, and take the necessary precautions before you leave. A free newsletter now available from the Health Care Abroad division of International Underwriters, Inc. (7653 Leesburg Pike, Falls Church, VA 22043), will help you do just that.

Recent issues of this quarterly publication have focused on the growing malaria risk, comparative medical costs in cities around the world, and which countries will treat visiting enrolled students under their own national health systems (Sweden and Japan won't; Britain, France, and Germany will, with some restrictions).

Several books are on the market which deal with travelers' health problems, and any good bookstore should have one. As for inoculations, the *Foreign Travel Immunization Guide,* by Dr. Hans H. Neumann, is updated periodically. It sells for $4.50 from the Medical Economics Company, Book Division, Oradell, NJ 07649. You can also get a lower-price 24-page pamphlet from the International Health Care Service of the New York Hospital–Cornell Medical Center, Box 210, 525 East 68th Street, New York, NY 10021. Send $1, and they'll mail you the pamphlet, which tells you about common travelers' diseases, inoculations, first aid kits, and the like. Also, the U.S. Department of Health, Education, and Welfare publishes a useful *Health Information for International*

Travel booklet. Check your local library for the latest edition.

Before going to a Third World country, pick up the little yellow booklet called the *International Certificates of Vaccination*. These are handed out by the U.S. Public Health Service, passport agencies, and the Superintendent of Documents, U.S. Government Printing Office, Washington, DC 20402. Find out from a doctor, clinic, or guidebook what inoculations you should have *according to the season* (cholera, for instance, appears only in the warm summer months). It may take weeks or months to get the full course of inoculation. Also, you can get up-to-date information about any country's political/health and related conditions from the State Department's Citizens Emergency Center in Washington (tel. 202/632-5225) between 8:15 a.m. and 5 p.m. weekdays.

Similar information can be gotten from the government tourist office of your particular destination.

FINDING A DOCTOR ABROAD: When you're overseas, your consulate can usually provide a list of doctors and dentists who speak English and who are used to treating travelers. In addition, several services provide lists of such physicians that you can obtain before you go. INTERMEDIC, 777 Third Avenue, New York, NY 10017, issues a directory listing physicians in over 200 cities around the world. The directory, and several other services such as information on inoculations recommended for foreign countries, is free to members. Membership costs $6 per year ($10 for families).

IAMAT (International Association for Medical Assistance for Travelers) provides its members (suggested contribution of $10 makes you a member) with a list of English-speaking doctors abroad, and also includes a helpful booklet with health care information for travelers. IAMAT is at 350 Fifth Ave., New York, NY 10007 (tel. 212/279-6465).

The American Express Company has compiled a directory of 3500 U.S.-certified doctors living abroad, which is on sale to its customers for $3.

MEDICINES, PRESCRIPTIONS: If you take medications regularly, take a supply which will last your trip, and also take a prescription giving the generic names of the drugs, since trade names vary in other countries. In the U.S., few pharmacies are allowed to honor an out-of-state prescription. Abroad, the drugs may not be available, or may have different names. However, if you know the generic names and dosages of the drugs, chances are good that you will be able to replace them if they are lost. The big drug companies are world wide concerns now, and the widely used drugs are sold everywhere and are familiar to pharmacists. The pharmacist may not have your specific drug, but may have very similar product which will do in an emergency.

You should also take along an extra pair of eyeglasses (or at the very least copies of your prescription). If you wear contact lenses, either take a pair of eyeglasses or another pair of lenses.

HEALTH INSURANCE: Most health insurance plans will cover at least part of the cost of a hospital stay abroad. Look at your policy and check with your employer to be sure. If you're not covered, call an insurance agent and get a short-term policy. Doctors and hospitals abroad often cost as much or more than at home, and visitors cannot depend on being treated gratis even though locals have a national health plan.

If you are taking a tour, do get insurance that includes coverage of return travel costs if you become ill and must stay behind when the tour moves on (otherwise, the sad fact is that you're on your own). Senior citizens be warned—Medicare will *not* cover medical expenses abroad, except in VERY limited circumstances in Mexico and Canada.

If a health care or other sudden emergency should arise when you're far from home, you can be prepared with a new kind of travel insurance plan called Assist-Card International. Its multi-faceted coverage includes health and hospital insurance (up to $3000); aid in finding lost luggage, legal help, assistance in finding and/or replacing lost travel documents; and emergency financial help (up to $1000). The plan also provides for emergency return-home costs for missed flights or deaths in the family.

Good strategic planning is the first requirement for a successful cost-effective trip. Failing to plan well is like forgetting your suitcase: you've got to get everything together on the road, in unfamiliar territory, perhaps at higher-than-home prices.

Depending on the length of your trip, plan costs can vary from $20 for five days to $120 for three months. Complete information is available from Assist-Card Corporation of America, 745 Fifth Avenue, New York, NY 10022 (from outside New York, toll free, call 800/221-4564).

Money

How to travel and carry money safely?

CASH: Cash is the easiest and also the most vulnerable. Which is better: to take a chance that some cash will be stolen, or to pay a gone-forever fee of 1% on your money converting it into travelers checks so that you can recover it if it is stolen? In some travel situations, there is simply no substitute for cash—in that tiny out-of-the-way café, or in the taxi or bus when you first arrive. It is wise to take along some cash, but not so much that you'd be in serious trouble if it were lost or stolen. Use it in cash-only situations—tipping, phone calls, to clinch a bargain deal in a local bazaar—but because travelers checks are a convenience and insurance against loss, have most of your travel funds in checks. Think carefully though, about how much, and where to buy the checks. Barclay's Bank, with branches in major American cities, does not charge. Deak Perera in New York City has a similar policy. Thomas Cook, the travel service that started the whole travelers check business a century ago, often promotes its checks by offering them for free. Note that the free checks offered are usually the company's and not American Express: that is, Thomas Cook's or Barclay's, both of which are perfectly acceptable throughout the world. So remember, always ask at your bank about free checks; also ask your travel or automobile club, or travel agent—they may have free check deals. That 1% fee is something that's easy to avoid; try not to pay it.

FREE TRAVELERS CHECKS: The banks and companies which issue travelers checks make money at both ends of the deal: they make you pay 1% for the checks, then they take the money you've given them and invest it at the going rate. No wonder they recommend that you "hold onto unused checks for future trips or emergencies." As long as you hold onto the check, they're making interest on your money.

This double-whammy is the reason some travelers check firms can afford to issue free checks.

Here's a little bonus: you usually get more foreign currency for your dollar travelers checks abroad than you do for an equivalent amount of dollar cash. If you cash a $100 travelers check in Mexico City, for instance, you may get 40 pesos for $1, or 4000 pesos total; for a $100 bill, you may only get 38 pesos for $1, or 3800 pesos total. By using travelers checks, you save 200 pesos—not much, but better than nothing. Why is this so? The cash dollars have to be sold or shipped back to the U.S. So, dealing with cash costs the banks more—the money they save on shipping costs is your bonus for using the travelers checks.

Always ask at your bank about free travelers checks, also ask your automobile club or travel agent—they may have free check deals. That 1% fee is something that's easy to avoid; try not to pay it.

PERSONAL CHECKS: Buying souvenirs at an Arab-run shop in Jerusalem, I asked the shopkeeper what form of payment would be preferable. Can you guess what he said? "Personal check, if you have one."

You may hear just the opposite of that at home, as in "No Personal Checks Accepted—Ever!" but in foreign countries, as a "wealthy" tourist, you're assumed to be good for your debts. Carry a number of personal checks with you when you travel abroad, but guard them as you would travelers checks. If they are lost or stolen, you should drop a note to your bank so they can be on the lookout for forgeries.

CREDIT CARDS: The bank credit card (MasterCard, VISA) is one of the traveler's most cost-effective tools. As with travelers checks, one must understand how the cards work in order to take advantage of them.

Most banks now charge an annual fee for their MasterCard and VISA cards. (An exception is European American Bank, which charges no annual fee.) As far as the banks are concerned, this fee is the icing on the cake, like the 1% travelers check fee. They can do without it, but it's nice to have. The banks' real concern is the 18% interest they earn on cash advances and on your unpaid monthly balance. The credit card companies, who manage the card transactions for the banks, get their cut from the hotels, gas stations, stores, and restaurants that honor the cards. These places pay a percentage (typically 3% or 4%, but sometimes as high as 8%) of the total of each credit card sale to the credit card company. The theory is that ease of payment—which the credit card offers—brings more customers and bigger sales, and so the hotel or restaurant loses nothing in the long run.

Actually, if you pay your hotel or restaurant bill in cash, you should pay less, because the credit card company doesn't take a percentage of the cash sale. If you pay for a $10 item with a $10 bill, the store keeps $10; if you pay by credit card, the store only keeps $9.20 to $9.70. A few places do offer discounts for cash customers (always ask). At the establishments which don't offer such a discount, use your credit card—you're going to pay for the convenience whether you use it or not, so use it. There's a bonus when you pay with plastic: when inflation is high, you earn money by deferring payment as long as possible. Charge a tankful of gas in Los Angeles—by the time the notice gets back to your bank in Toronto and appears on your monthly statement, and the due date rolls around, it may be six weeks since you bought—and used—the gas. In effect, you've had an interest-free loan for 1½ months, while the money with which you will pay for the gas was earning big interest elsewhere. On overseas trips the saving may be even greater, as it may take months for a sales notice to reach your bank from Athens, Tunis, or Singapore.

The bank credit card is one of the traveler's most cost-effective tools.

However, keep in mind that it's not *always* advantageous to pay by credit card. If exchange rates are fluctuating wildly you may lose some money by paying the bill a month after the actual business transaction, depending on which way the currency is moving. Also, in times of high inflation or when the dollar is falling you may be advised to book and prepay accommodations, car rentals, airfares, etc. Those travelers who did so in 1981–82 were caught at a disadvantage when the dollar began to rise strongly. The independent traveler who was able to pay on the spot in local currency was able to reap the greatest advantage from the dollar's spectacular recovery.

This mini-treatise on credit cards is important because today those little bank cards are honored throughout the world. You'll be surprised how often you'll use them, and each time you do you'll be getting a discount—provided, of course, that you always pay your monthly bill on time, in full. Wipe out the balance and they charge you no interest.

In many Third World countries, only the more expensive establishments may honor the cards, but you can still benefit from the cash advance provisions.

Walk into a bank abroad, flash your bank credit card (MasterCard or VISA), and you can usually get several hundred dollars in five minutes. Some banks honor both cards, some one card or the other; often the card will have a different name ("Bancomatico," "Access," "Eurocard," etc.). The name doesn't matter. What matters is that you get your money *at the best exchange rate, with no exchange fee* (in most cases). However, you should be aware that cash advances cost 18%, starting as soon as the bank receives notice of them. The only way you can avoid paying this interest is to pay off the entire balance in your account as soon as the bank receives notice of the cash advance. Actually, this is possible—if you have two credit cards. Use one card for buying things, and use the other one for cash advances. Whenever you take a cash advance, mail off a check for the same amount to your credit card bank. The check will cancel out the cash advance. You don't need to send a bill along with your check. All the bank needs to credit your account is your name, address, card name, account number, and the check. The bank accepts the check as payment, cancels the cash advance, and your money continues to earn interest for another two weeks until the check clears!

One last suggestion: get both cards. In the U.S., a place that takes MasterCard almost always takes VISA, too. But it's different abroad. In Canada, lots of places accept only VISA; in Paris, the convenient banks accept VISA, and only a few take MasterCard. This is changing, but for the time being, have both. If you can get one, you can get two. It's silly, but then, so much is!

What about American Express? The American Express card carries status, high credit facilities, and many little extras such as free travel insurance, hotel reservation confirmation facilities, etc. Also, interest is not added to outstanding accounts until the second month a charge is billed. But it is not a money-saver. It costs more in fees, and it often demands higher percentages from the hotels and merchants who honor it; this means that many times only the more expensive places, which have higher mark-ups, can afford to honor the card. In general, the bank cards (Master-Card, VISA) are more widely accepted.

Passports

You can save yourself $5 by renewing your passport. If you have no passport, have never had one, and are therefore getting one for the first time, you will have to go to a post office or passport office, fill out a white form, take an oath, and sign the form in the presence of the clerk. You give the clerk two copies of a recent photo of yourself (2 inches square), and $15, and your passport will be mailed to you.

There are U.S. Passport Agencies in Boston, Chicago, Honolulu, Houston, Los Angeles, Miami, New Orleans, New York City, Philadelphia, San Francisco, Seattle, Stamford, Conn., and Washington, D.C. In other places, you submit your application and take the oath before a postal clerk, Federal or State court clerk, or probate court judge or clerk. Take along proof of U.S. citizenship and those all-important photos.

The savings come when you get your second, third, or fourth passport. These days, a passport is good for five years, and is not renewable, strictly speaking— instead of a renewal, you get a whole new passport with a new number. However, if you obtained your old passport after you were 18 years of age, and if it is less than eight years since that old passport was issued, you are allowed to use the Passport Office's pink form, available at any post office. When you use the pink form, the fee is only $10, which you must enclose with your old passport and two new copies of a recent photo.

Do you need a passport? For most of the world, yes. For travel to Canada, Mexico, many Caribbean and Central and South American countries, no. To these places you can use some other weighty document which is proof of identity: a birth certificate or voter registration card is often sufficient (but a driver's license or college ID is not). However, nothing proves your identity quickly and powerfully like a passport. It makes matters like cashing travelers checks and checking in for flights very simple.

Phrase Books and Dictionaries

These items are really only necessary for the adventurous traveler. During a weekend in Montreal, a week in Mexico City and Acapulco, you will probably meet mostly those locals who speak English. For a longer trip, a good phrase book helps you open doors, make smiles, win friends, understand what's going on. The series put out by Editions Berlitz (Berlitz Publications) is widely available, inexpensive, and filled with cultural descriptions as well as words and phrases. A good phrase book like this makes a dictionary unnecessary.

Student and Youth Hostel Cards

Another thing to do before heading out, whether you travel at home or abroad, is to obtain a student ID card and/or a Youth Hostel card. *Age is no barrier* in many cases. To become a member of the American Youth Hostels, Inc., a person over 18 years of age merely pays a higher fee ($14 per year). With your Youth Hostel Card, you can stay at inexpensive youth hostels all over the world. Buy your hostel membership at any hostel, or contact American Youth Hostels, Inc., National Headquarters, 1332 I St., NW, Washington, DC 20005 (tel. 202/347-3125, or toll-free 800/424-9426); in Canada, contact the Canadian Hosteling Association, 333 River Rd., Vanier, ON K1L 8B9 (tel. 613/746-3844).

To obtain the International Student Identity Card (ISIC), you must be a full-time high school or university student, and you must send documentary proof of such status such as a letter from the school principal, dean, or registrar, sealed with the official school seal. Many college campuses have an office which issues the ISIC. If yours doesn't, contact the Council on International Educational Exchange (CIEE), 205 East 42nd St., New York, NY 10017 (tel. 212/661-1414), or the CIEE offices in Boston, Miami, Seattle, San Francisco, Berkeley, Los Angeles, or San Diego. Note that age is no barrier to obtaining a student card; you can be of any age, but you must be a full-time high school or college student.

With these two cards, a wealth of inexpensive accommodations, flights, meals, and things to do is opened up to you.

Visas, Tourist Cards, and Permits

For foreign countries, there are many items you may want to obtain in advance. When you travel to Third World countries or Eastern Europe, it's often necessary to have a visa or at least a "Tourist Card." Obtaining these permits-to-enter is usually easiest in the U.S. or Canada, with less bureaucratic hassle and fewer payoffs. Think of it this way: the Consular Officer of Upper Slobovia, sitting in the embassy in Washington or the consulate in New York or Los Angeles, fills requests for Slobovian visas by mail. He's happy to be in North America (most Third World officials are), he likes his job, he wants to appear efficient and modern-minded to us, and so he does his best to fulfill your request without any hassle.

Depending upon the Third World country you plan to visit, you may be able to obtain visas and Tourist Cards at the border or upon landing in the airport. But consider the position of the Slobovian Immigration Officer there: probably underpaid, often envious of foreigners—the officer has a lot of incentive to hit you for a bribe. After all, the situation is urgent: your bus or train is about to depart for the interior, or you've just landed and are not about to climb back on a plane rather than pay a small bribe. He's got you. With a visa and/or a Tourist Card already in your pocket, you're in a much stronger position to get through formalities quickly and cheaply.

This advice extends to special-interest permits as well: want to go hunting, or digging in the ruins, or hiking in outlying areas? You'll often need a permit for these activities, and you'll *always* need a permit to import firearms. Get these things in advance, and allow plenty of time for the bureaucracy to churn.

6

Packing to Save Money

It is possible to travel with no more luggage than an airline flight bag or large purse. People who travel this way are not unwashed barbarians. They are the most liberated people on the road.

Until my very own sister-in-law went on vacation with three monster American Touristers packed like sausages, I thought this dinosaur mode of travel had disappeared from the earth. I was so accustomed to traveling with only one small shoulder bag, I actually thought all those huge suitcases at the airport baggage claim were owned by business travelers and immigrants moving with large families.

You can take lots of luggage, sure. Be prepared to pay for the privilege in time, labor, worry, and inconvenience—not to mention real money.

What are the bare essentials? Well, my brother used to put a toothbrush in his pocket and head out to the airport. He didn't even weigh himself down with *money*. Staying with friends, borrowing toothpaste, razors, and soap, wrapping in a towel while a friend took his clothes to the laundromat. . . . It is indeed possible to pack nothing at all. But for most of us it is just too much of a hassle to spend all our time making do.

You *can* pack lightly. Instead of starting with the checklist (two shirts, three underpants, etc.), do it backwards: start with your bag.

BAGS AND BACKPACKS

Rule of thumb: your bag for a month's travel (or less) in a warmish climate should be small enough to carry on the airplane and stow under the seat, and you should be able to carry it by a shoulder strap for a 20-minute walk without having to put it down (you get to change shoulders, though). The bag itself should be light but strong.

If you must have some more space, *do not* buy a large bag! Buy a second shoulder bag, or a backpack. These days, bags and packs come in such an amazing assortment of styles that you can have whatever you dream of. The best pack is one that converts to a suitcase for hand-carrying: the shoulder straps tuck in here, a carrying handle pops out of there. Yes, such bags exist, and their tidy appearance sets them well apart from the stock image of the ragged, youthful pack-toting vagabond.

WHAT TO TAKE

It would be impossible to give a useful checklist of what to take, because that depends so much upon where you go and what you plan to do when you get there. Going to Acapulco for sun and sea? You can get by with jeans, shirt and bathing suit. Are you interested in discos? Then you'd better throw in snazzy slacks, too.

When you make up your own list, keep these points in mind: Three tops and two pairs of slacks constitute a basic travel wardrobe. You can do perfectly well with this minimum. One pair of slacks should be blue jeans, or something similarly informal; the other pair should be more formal. As for the tops, have one shirt or blouse, one jersey or turtleneck, and a T-shirt. The T-shirt is also your undershirt, pyjamas, and beach top. Coats and jackets? Take only those you can wear on your back—if cold sets in, use the simple technique of layering—a T-shirt under an overblouse under your all-purpose jacket or coat.

You simply cannot travel heavy and travel cheaply at the same time. It is possible to travel with no more luggage than an airline flight bag or large purse.

Women who simply cannot subsist on such super-basic informality should pack one dress—or skirt and top that looks like a dress—that does not need ironing, two or three blouses, two slacks or skirts, for a total of three interchangeable outfits. Scarves can work wonders dressing up the simplest pants outfit if need be. Take only two pairs of shoes, one very comfy and informal, and one dress-up pair. Take lotions, creams, shampoo, and conditioner in small plastic bottles scrounged for the purpose (big spenders can buy them in variety or drug stores). Instead of curlers, take a single curling iron; it's a bit more work to use the curling iron, but it's lighter and smaller.

"Oh, that's fine, but I saw a nice little travel iron. I'll buy that, and then take clothes which may need ironing." Heed: irons are made of *iron*; and I have never yet encountered a travel iron that did the job well, easily, and simply. You're much better off taking wrinkle-free clothes.

This minimum is bound to frighten you: "How will I ever get along for two months on that small wardrobe?" Instead of fear, your actual experience is more likely to yield pleasure. A spartan wardrobe gives you the freedom of not having to worry about clothes, or what to wear. More important, it gives you the truly priceless freedom of easy unencumbered traveling. If you have lots of room in your shoulder bag after it's packed, throw in one more shirt and one more pair of slacks or a skirt.

As for other items, they depend on climate. You will almost always need a sweater, even in Egypt where the desert gets very cool at night. The amount of underclothing you take depends directly on the climate. To a hot, dry climate, take very little as it will dry within an hour after you wash it. To a damp, cold climate, take more, because it may take two days to dry.

Do not take clothes that are brand new, especially shoes. Break in clothes before you go, and break in new shoes well. A new shoe not only rubs, it exercises different muscles. Until those new muscles acquire tone, your legs will be sore. You don't want sore legs on a trip where you will be required to walk half the day—and you walk that much no matter how or where you travel.

If you've forgotten something, or if you find the basic wardrobe much too confining, buy something abroad. It will probably be more expensive, but it's nice to buy exotic clothes.

Plan to wash your own clothes. You may not end up washing everything—those blue jeans, for example. But do provide yourself with the capability—they say even President Truman washed out his own underclothes when he traveled. It's quick and convenient, and in some countries it is so expensive to have things laundered that you'd be shocked. For more tips on doing your own laundry, see p. 222.

The minimum number of garments (shirts, trousers, underwear) is two: "wash one, wear one."

PACKING TECHNIQUE

And now the actual packing. Start out with a liberal supply of plastic Baggies—the ziplock kind. Fold each garment neatly so it will fit into a Baggie. Force out all the air before locking it, and the dress or whatever will survive for up to a week virtually wrinkle-free. One pair of pants with top can also fit into a Baggie. Underwear goes in another and so on. Cosmetics, vitamins, camera, and film all go into a separate plastic bag.

Your bag, for a month's travel (or less) in a warmish climate, should be small enough to stow under the seat of an airplane, and you should be able to carry it by a shoulder strap for a twenty-minute walk without having to put it down.

Surrounded by all those neatly zipped Baggies, you're ready to pack your bag or suitcase. Put shoes in the corners, line the sides with toiletries, then place all the other clothes upright—like files in a filing cabinet. Not only will they fit into a minimum of space, they'll be easy to identify and pull out without having to rumple up everything else in the bag. If you're using a rucksack or duffle bag, use the outside zipper pockets for documents, paperbacks and the like (as long as you're taking the bag on the plane).

With any luck, by following these rather simple rules, you'll wind up with everything you need for a comfortable happy trip—and you'll be the character with the smug expression walking jauntily past the baggage carousel.

PART TWO

How to Cut Transportation Costs

Choosing your transportation requires clear thinking. It helps to follow in the mental footsteps of Descartes, who stripped away superstitions, traditions, and stereotypes and looked straight at the thing itself.

I used to think that driving from Boston to New York was the cheapest way to get there, because gas and tolls cost me only $40, and the train or bus cost $60, the plane $90 (round trip). I wasn't looking clearly, though. I spent 10½ hours driving, my car got towed once ($100), I was forced to pay $15 to $20 for a few hours' parking in Manhattan, and I still ended up taking some taxis because it wasn't worth taking the car out of the lot for transportation within the city. I could have saved time, energy, and money by leaving the driving to someone else.

All this was uncovered when I decided to look closely and clearly at what I was doing, rather than relying on old notions or vague preferences.

In Vienna, I rented a car from a small local agency that had lower rates than the big companies—or so I thought until they tacked on charges for cleaning the interior, washing the exterior, "service inspection," "license fee," etc., etc. Which price was truly lower?

Having learned from my Vienna experience, I got to Marrakech, and instead of renting a car I searched for a place that rented motorcycles. The rental was totally satisfactory, and cost one-quarter of what a car would have. In this case, I had looked clearly at my transportation needs, used a bit of creativity, and come out way ahead. No nasty surprises.

To help you avoid nasty surprises, and to save you money, the next few chapters will examine the various transportation modes available to you.

7

Unscrambling the Airfares

Two extremely important points to remember: *air travel today is basically a real bargain; and, it is a commodity business much like the hotel business.*

On the first point: I first crossed the Atlantic in 1966. I paid $305 for a round-trip charter flight between Boston and London. Ten years later, after wild inflation of the dollar, the price was considerably *lower.* In terms of constant dollars, the price was ridiculously low. Jumbo jets, better engines, mass marketing, ingenious scheduling, and ticket sales plans have all reduced the costs of flying. Like telephone service, flying is one of the great bargains of the time. Those with only the standard two-week vacation appreciate fully what a valuable bargain air service is.

I hasten to add that this applies mostly to North American–based flights. In many parts of the world, conservative regulations and inefficient business practices have kept airfares unconscionably high.

On the second point: Think of an airplane flight in these terms. The plane costs a lot of money to buy, to store, to maintain. The most efficient and profitable way to use an airplane is to keep it flying as much as possible. When it's flying, it incurs certain expenses: fuel, crew, landing fees, wear and tear. These costs are virtually the same whether the plane is full or empty. If the plane takes off with an empty seat, that empty seat is a symbol of revenue lost forever, because for exactly the same costs, the airplane could have made more dollars by finding someone to pay something to fill that seat. Naturally, the airline will want to get as much money as possible for the seat. Two weeks before flight time, chances are good it can get a full fare. But what about two hours before flight time? Or 30 minutes? Chances are now close to zero for getting a full fare, and near zero for getting any money at all. Soon that seat will be airborne, having earned $0. Hence the airlines and the charter operators have created a variety of ticket categories and special gimmicks to sell their seats.

In fact, all is chaos in the realm of air travel, as deregulation of the airline industry has opened up the marketplace to full-fledged price competition. New airlines are springing up overnight, offering promotional fares and special deals to capture business from the established lines. This is good for you and me because we can benefit from some incredibly low fares—trips at prices that make an airline executive limp with despair. But it's bad because it's confusing. The neat and tidy system of past years is gone, and one can no longer depend on many services once taken for granted. You may have to pay a penalty if you change your reservations or cancel your ticket. You may not be able to check your bags straight through to your destination if you are flying on more than one line—indeed, you may have to buy several tickets rather than just one ticket with several coupons. The friendly airline reservations agent may no longer let you know about flights by other lines. And the check-in clerk may not accept the ticket of another airline in exchange for his own airline's.

In such a situation, the latest up-to-date information is of the greatest importance, so scour the travel publications and newspapers, consult a good travel agent, and use your telephone. I can't predict the special price-war fares that come and go with the seasons, but I can fill you in on the *categories* of air transportation and airfares available to you. These categories—in more or less ascending order of price are: charters; standby fares; "cheap airlines"; promotions and APEX fares; and then the regular fares (economy, business, and first class).

CHARTERS

New rules allow airlines to intermix charter and regular passengers on the same flight, and so the person sitting near you may well have paid a radically different fare from what you paid. A charter is a sort of "group APEX," whereby a travel agent or tour operator gets together a group of people all going to the same destination at the same time. Savings are great because such a group has great bargaining power with the airlines. Flexibility on a charter is nil: you make your arrangements, pay the price, and then go. If you don't go, you lose your money and your chance unless you've made trip insurance arrangements. But charters often offer the cheapest means of travel. Although charter activity lapsed somewhat in the late '70s, the 1980s seem poised for a resurgence in charter travel, especially trans-Atlantic. For example, the Davis Agency, headquartered at Century Building in Arlington, Virginia, will be operating charters in 1982 from nearly a dozen U.S. cities (ranging from Los Angeles to St. Louis, to Chicago, to New York) and going to Frankfurt, Madrid, and Amsterdam, at round-trip rates of around $520 to $560 in the height of the summer season. The official U.S. student travel organization, the Council on International Educational Exchange (CIEE), 205 East 42nd Street, New York, NY 10017, offers weekly charters from New York to Paris each year for very low prices. Other charter operators will be offering all kinds of programs.

Sources of Charter Information

Where do you ferret out the dates, departure cities, and prices for charter transportation? The most obvious way is to consult the Sunday travel section of your local newspaper, or, if you live in a small town, the Sunday travel section of the nearest large-city newspaper. Any major charter program will certainly be advertised.

Should I sign up for a tour? Of course you should. Often there is no cheaper way to get airfare and accommodations, even if you make all the arrangements yourself. And remember, you can usually buy air only or else toss out the land package and still save money.

A far more comprehensive source of information is the monthly *JaxFax*, magazine of the air chartering industry, published from 280 Tokeneke Rd., Darien, CT 06820 (tel. 203/655-8746). Travel agents all over the nation subscribe to *JaxFax* for its listings of all charters scheduled to depart this country in the next six months. Subscription price is $9 a year, but you don't have to subscribe. Simply visit a nearby travel agency and ask courteously whether you may peruse their current copy of *JaxFax* on the premises. Since the same travel agent can then book you aboard that charter and earn a commission, he or she will usually be happy to oblige.

TOURS AND PACKAGES

The perennial question: Should I sign up for a tour? Of course you should. Often, there is no cheaper way to get airfare and accommodations, even if you make all the arrangements yourself.

And remember, you can often purchase air only and still save an incredible amount over the regular fares by doing so. Even if you can't purchase air only, you can always toss out the land package (you'll be paying for it), make your own accommodations and meals arrangements, and still save money. Here's why. Most of the land packages are negotiated at incredibly low prices, so that even if you add the cost of the land package into your overall airfare you'll still be paying less than if you took a regular airfare (or sometimes even a discounted airfare). So don't look down your nose at the package tour; if you have limited time, often you can't beat it for value.

If you do buy the whole package, look carefully at what you do in fact get for your money. Read the brochure carefully, including all the fine print. Ask friends if they've taken a tour with the outfit you're thinking of traveling with. You might even go so far as to check with the hotel of your choice about what kind of room you can expect. If you're promised beachfront accommodations, make sure that you're not going to be staying at a hotel miles from the beach with just a glimpse of the sea off in the distance. These things can happen. Also ask what kind of food will be served at mealtime. You don't want dried up veal chops and other American fare. And remember, many of the sightseeing offerings, nightlife packages, and other little bonuses may *seem* to be included in the price. Often they're not. Make sure—be a smart consumer.

If you still don't get satisfactory treatment, then you can inform your Better Business Bureau and the consumer department of the U.S. Tour Operators Association, 211 E. 51st St., Suite 4-B, New York, NY 10022. Better to make sure you'll have a good trip before you go!

STANDBY FARES

One must be careful of standby fares these days. The concept of standby travel is a useful one for passengers and airlines alike; if they have an empty seat at the last moment, you get it—at the last moment—at a bargain price. Both are happy.

But the hazards may be greater than you realize. I once flew on a major airline to London in October and was assured that I would have no trouble getting a standby seat back to New York. After all, it was off season; I could fly back midweek; it should be no trouble. However, when it came time for my return I checked with the airline; there were no seats available that day on any airline, and it looked very likely that there would be no seat available for a few days, if the computer was doing its job correctly. Thanks to an ingenious airline reservationist I was able to get onto a flight bound for Washington (for which I had to pay some additional money). From Washington I had to make my own way. I wound up renting a car, which cost a fortune and was exhausting. If I had opted to stay in London though, I would have had to pay for accommodations, meals and living expenses for who knows how many days. So beware. In my experience you're better planning ahead to take advantage of one of the many discount fares available if you book in advance.

Moreover, when it comes to going to Europe standby fares are available (with one minor exception) only to and from London.

Whatever you do, make sure that you're willing and well-prepared to hazard all the risks outlined above before heading out to the airport as a standby.

THE "CHEAP AIRLINES"

Deregulation of the aviation industry has caused several new "cheap airlines" to emerge on both the domestic and the world scene. Most notable among the domestics are: People Express, New York Air, Midway Airlines, Air Florida, Mid-Pacific Air. The most notable new international carriers include: Capitol Airways, Metro Air, TransAmerica Airlines, and World Airways. All of them offer airfares that are considerably lower than flag carriers and major airlines.

These "new" airlines are, in the main, the formerly so-called "supplemental carriers" that once were limited by CAB regulations to the operation of charter flights only, but now can—and do—operate scheduled flights almost anywhere they choose.

And, incidentally, the only thing "cheap" about these airlines is their price structure, not their service or standards. They fly the same planes as the major carriers, adhere to the same standards, and usually hire the same caliber of personnel. A common error made by some timid travelers is to assume that a lesser-known carrier is somehow less safe than a better-known one; there isn't an iota of statistical evidence to support that belief.

There's a reason why Pan American hired C. Edward Acker, former chairman of Air Florida, to run their currently ailing airline.

More of these airlines will surely appear. Keep an eye out for them and their advertisements in the newspapers, magazines and travel industry media.

PROMOTIONAL FARES

These are where the action is. Airlines entering new routes don't price by cost, but by undercutting everybody else. Often the promotional fares will have a fancy advertising name. Most of the time, the airline will tell you right out that their fare is the lowest. The airline certainly does not intend to keep the fare that low after it has built up its clientele. But for the time being, it's a goldmine.

Two points to remember: air travel today is basically a real bargain; and, it is a commodity business much like the hotel business.

The airlines are in fact using all kinds of imaginative gambits to attract customers. Here are just two examples of the kind of campaigns that you might encounter. Right now, early in 1982, Eastern Airlines is offering an unlimited mileage ticket that entitles the passenger to fly on Eastern's U.S. routes (including to the Bahamas, Bermuda, and San Juan) for 21 days for a low price of $540 each for two traveling together or $640 if you're alone. The ticket must be purchased 14 days in advance. For about $80 more you can fly *all* of Eastern's routes including to Mexico and the Caribbean.

As another example, Pan Am's Triangle Fare enables a passenger traveling from New York City to

California (San Francisco or Los Angeles) to fly to Miami as well for $9 more than the basic New York–California coach fare.

To keep pace with all these developments and to ensure that you're first in line, examine all the newspapers, magazines, and travel industry publications for advertisements and announcements. There's a fare somewhere for you.

APEX AND SUPER-APEX

APEX (Advanced-Purchase Excursion) tickets are the cost-conscious traveler's dependable friend. Costing about 25% less than economy (40% less than business), APEX fares must be booked and paid for 21 to 30 days in advance, and you must stay at your destination at least seven but no more than 60 or 90 days, depending upon destination. You pay a penalty (usually $50) if you cancel; no stopovers are permitted. Most APEX tickets are transferrable between airlines, though. Super-APEX fares have the same terms as APEX, but they're priced even lower. In effect, they are loss-leaders which make good advertising. Go after them early, as the seats are few in number and quickly sold. Round trip only.

THE REGULAR FARES

Economy Class

This is the lowest fare that still allows you freedom to change your mind. No advanced-purchase requirements, no charge for cancellation or change, and you can transfer the ticket to another airline. For a small extra fee, you can get a single stopover along the way. One way or round trip.

Business Class

Each airline has its own name for this service, which offers a few advantages over economy fare for a little bit more money. In effect, you get the booties for much less. The valuable part of this fare is the right to unlimited stopovers enroute to your destination, and when returning. This feature is of great value to the business traveler, and may prove the cheapest way for you to fly, as well. One way or round trip.

First-Class

Very nice, but very pricey. You get to change your mind and your flight for up to a year. But the fare is over twice as much as for an economy flight, which means those little furry booties and that glass of champagne are by no means "free." In effect, you are paying hand-made-leather-shoe prices for booties.

SOME FINAL FLYING TIPS

Don't forget the old standard 25% night-flight discount.

Remember, also, that you'll usually pay a supplement to fly on weekends. Note the exception: the shuttles between Boston–New York–Washington; special reduced excursion fares are offered on weekends. Other commuter routes may provide similar weekend opportunities.

Often you will be flying overseas to your destination. Once there, you will most likely want to travel either by train or car, or some other means of surface transportation because air transportation costs are prohibitive. For example, in Europe inter-city air travel is so costly that you're definitely better off on the ground.

8

Cutting Car Costs

If you have time, and want freedom from schedules and routes, and are not traveling alone, then going by car makes good sense. Don't make the mistake I did, though. Work out the *true cost,* in time, effort, and money. You may be unpleasantly surprised.

COMPUTING THE *REAL* COST

The U.S. Government computes the cost of operating a private motor vehicle at 20¢ to 25¢ per mile, plus tolls and parking fees. A dollar every four miles; $10 every 40 miles; $100 every 400 miles; $200 for 800 miles—but you can fly from New York to Los Angeles (3000 miles) for less than $200. Does the plane look expensive now? Even with two people, and thus a plane fare of $400, the equivalent cost of driving from New York to L.A. would be $600 to $750, plus parking and tolls, at the government's figures.

As they say, "Your mileage may vary," and if you have a small, fuel-efficient car you may do better.

Rental cars are also very expensive, particularly abroad. Several years ago I rented a car in England. I knew that in the car rental business they handed out 10% discounts all the time, so I offered to rent the car for a week, rather than just two days, if they gave me the "10% commercial discount." (I planned to rent it for a week in any case.) I got the discount, and my total cost for the car was still $50 a day—and that's in England, where you can't drive very far before you hit water. I rented the very cheapest car. Gas costs $3 per gallon in England.

Keep these points in mind:

Four or more people sharing a car is budget travel. One or two people sharing a car is luxury travel.

Figure car expenses realistically and completely. Here are items you must include:

Fuel, at 5¢ to 10¢ per mile (30 mpg to 15 mpg)
Oil, tires, maintenance, wear-and-tear, insurance, etc.
Parking and tolls
Highway food and lodging costs

For a rental car, you must figure:

Daily or weekly rental charge
Mileage charge (this and fuel are the highest charges!)
Full insurance charge
Taxes (often very high; 20% is not unusual abroad)
Fuel
Parking and tolls
Pick-up and delivery charges (if you use these services)
Stamp taxes, "document fees" or "execution fees"

CAR RENTAL SAVINGS

You may think that the car rental companies' rates are ironclad. Really they're not. In fact, all sorts of deals are possible—discounts for longer rentals, unlimited mileage or a certain number of free miles, free return delivery ("rent here, leave there"). The amount is limited only by demand, and by your ingenuity. This sort of thing goes on all the time wherever a company is stuck with a surplus of cars. If you don't believe it, stand near a rental counter in an airport sometime. You may be astounded to find that the rental company does not have ironclad rates at all. Instead, each person who shows up at the counter will get a rate based on his *expectations* and previous arrangements. I saw a man come up to a rental counter with an open magazine in his hand. "Look at the price they're giving on the West Coast," he said, and showed the clerk an advertisement for that company's cars. "But that's a different market," the clerk answered, "and we have a different rate structure here." Clutching his magazine and smiling, the potential customer replied, "Well, a car is a car, and if you can do it there I'll bet you can do it here." A minute later the clerk was on the phone to a supervisor, checking the inventory of available cars and getting permission to work out a special deal: the low price, or a price one dollar higher than the low price, or a fancier car for the standard-car price, or free miles.

Where and What to Rent

No matter what car rental company you choose to rent from you will always save money away from the airport—sometimes as much as 50% off the Hertz/Avis rate if you go to one of the "other" companies. Obviously, rental offices at airports have very high overheads and a captive audience. The business traveler can afford to rent there; the well-heeled character or the tired lazy traveler will want to fall into a car as they get off the plane—but smart travelers will want to rent from the offices downtown away from the airport. The companies that don't have offices at the airport will sometimes have courtesy shuttles to and from the airport. Again, it pays to investigate—the inconvenience may be minimal, the savings well worth it.

You may think that the car rental companies' rates are ironclad. They're not. In fact, all sorts of deals are possible.

Besides comparison shopping among the rental companies, you should know that rental cars are cheaper in some countries than in others. Of course, if you are only visiting one country this has little relevance, but if you are going on an extensive trip through several European countries you should stop and think and discover where you will be better off renting the car. For example, at this time car rentals are cheapest in Denmark, Spain, Portugal, and Luxembourg. Avoid Switzerland, if possible.

Sales tax (VAT) rates also vary considerably, from 2.4% in Spain to 31% in Austria; you may have to check with the appropriate consulate for this information.

Different countries obviously also have different types of cars available and also varying gas prices. In Europe gas is often double the U.S. price; therefore you are much better off with a small car that gets good gas mileage. Remember, you don't have to sacrifice too much in space and comfort to obtain this savings—in Britain, for example, you may regard their Mini Minor as too small and too uncomfortable. Opt instead for a compact like the Ford Fiesta and you'll get space, comfort, and almost comparable mileage.

Discounts and Special Promotions

All car rental companies have busy periods and slack periods: their busiest time is Monday through Thursday when traveling businesspeople require their services and will pay highly for them. Slack periods are Friday to Monday, and therefore most companies offer special weekend packages that grant substantial discounts off the daily rates. The package may demand a two- or three-day minimum rental; it may offer some free mileage—100 or 200 miles. Even if the package does not include any free mileage, it will still represent a substantial savings depending on the distance you travel.

No matter what car rental company you choose to rent from, you will always save money by renting away from the airport.

Certain destinations generate more and greater discounts than others. A very popular destination and the resultant competition for business will give rise to all kinds of special promotions—fly/drive packages, no drop-off charges, etc. Florida is a prime example. Here you'll pay a fraction of what you'd pay in New York for a car rental. Sleuth out such special deals from newspapers, airlines, tour operators, the media, friends, and take advantage of them. Don't wait until you get to your destination and hope to obtain a discounted car. More often than not, you'll be unlucky.

Always figure out which package/deal is better for you. Find out what the daily rate plus mileage charge is and what, let's say, the weekend package charge is and what it gives you. Compare the prices based on how far you intend to drive and choose accordingly.

In general, try to avoid renting on a daily basis unless you're only going a very short distance. One of the highest costs of any daily car rental bill is the mileage charge which may be as high as 12¢ per mile. If you travel 500 miles in a three-day rental, you'll pay a whopping $60 in addition to the daily rate which, let's say, is $26. That's $138 plus insurance, sales tax, and, of course, fuel costs. If you do anticipate driving long distances your best value for money is the unlimited mileage weekly packages. Rent for one, two, or three weeks and you'll pay a flat sum and avoid those high mileage charges.

Sometimes, you can even get an additional discount if you book in advance. For example, I recently rented a car for a week from Hertz at London airport. Because I knew my schedule, and had planned far enough ahead to book three weeks in advance, I received a 50% discount off the regular unlimited mileage weekly package. Instead of paying $240 I paid $120.

Do shop around for car rentals. Read the advertisements and use your telephone. Most of the major outfits have toll-free numbers and by calling you can accurately compute the costs and determine which is the most cost-effective deal for you. Remember, deals vary from company to company.

Personal Discounts

Always ask about personal discount cards. Most companies have them. Tilden of Canada has a variety of them—blue cards, red cards, each bestowing some form of discount or privilege.

The company you work for has probably arranged special discounts for employees with specific car rental firms. Check with your personnel department and then check with the car rental firm. In certain situations you may be better off taking a rental company's special discounts, weekend packages, unlimited mileage deals, etc., rather than your own company discount. Always compute what is best for you.

Many car owners are members of AAA. Did you know that AAA membership entitles you to discounts at Hertz and Avis? The discounts vary, depending on where you rent. A membership card is not enough to deliver the discount though; you must show a special discount card. Make sure you have it.

Budget, Thrifty, Econo-Car, etc.

That brings me to another point. We all know the advantages of the two giants Hertz and Avis—new cars, good service, instant substitution of another car if yours breaks down. In short, all the advantages you'd expect an international network of offices to automatically deliver. But you pay for that. Next time you consider renting a car, check the prices of the "other" firms: Budget, Thrifty, Dollar, Econo-Car, and other similar companies, both here and abroad.

Their company policies demand that they keep their prices below those of the big companies. That is, if Hertz charges $32 a day, Dollar will charge $29 a day. If Hertz comes down to $29, Dollar will drop to $26. If you want to check the rates in the city or area you intend to visit, go to any travel agent and ask to see their copy of *Ground Transportation Services*. Compare the rates and then follow up with phone calls on the companies' toll-free numbers just to make sure that you have up-to-the minute information on prices, discounts, etc.

The Locals

Besides Hertz and Avis and the budget car rental companies, there are always a number of smaller, local companies that rent cars at much lower rates. Although you may find their location inconvenient, their cars perhaps a little older, their services not so extensive, their rates may still appeal to you. Again, check it out. Compute the overall costs and choose accordingly. Some of these small local firms will in fact pick you up and ferry you back to the airport for free. The Tourist offices can usually provide you with details about the local car rental companies. Write ahead or call. Investigate. It always pays.

Rent a Wreck

The last few years have seen the emergence in North America of rental firms which offer older-model cars for use in restricted areas, at greatly reduced charges. It would be easy to be misled by their innovative, but less-than-appealing names: Rent-A-Wreck, Rent-A-Fender-Bender, etc., but the truth is that in every case, the cars are maintained in excellent shape. While they don't have that new-car shine, they're probably better looking than that second car you bought for the kids. Most are between two and five years old, and all firms pay for road service, should you need it. Insurance is provided by almost all firms, some at a slight additional fee, and most will accept major credit cards. On the minus side, there's almost always a restriction on the driving radius, there are *no* one-way rentals, none has facilities at airports, and few provide airport transportation. Also, not all are open seven days a week around the clock, which means you must pick up and return cars during specified office hours. Still, if your holiday is centered on one city and environs, the savings in rental will more than offset any airport taxis and other small inconveniences.

If you're ready for the risks and potential hazards, then you can rent a car right now in New York for $20 a day, for only $10 a day in Los Angeles, both including 100 free miles a day. Most of these companies are locally owned and operated. To find them go to the library and check the Yellow Pages or else contact the local tourist offices and convention bureaus. Rent-A-Wreck, however, is a national franchise organization and you can find the location you need by calling 213/208-7712 (in Los Angeles) or toll-free 800/421-7253 nationwide. Charges vary from place to place, as well as types and sizes of cars offered. A similar outfit is Ugly Duckling (toll-free information, 800/854-3380), and there are many other smaller ones, too.

A Note on Car Rental Insurance

When you rent a car you will be asked to initial two boxes. One box usually refers to collision damage waiver; the other to personal insurance coverage. Always accept the collision damage waiver. By doing so, you will *NOT* have to pay the first $250 (or whatever the deductible) of any repairs in the event of an accident, provided you do not abridge the contract in any way, e.g., by allowing a driver who is not named in the contract to drive, towing another car, etc.

It's up to you whether or not you pay for the personal accident coverage. Most people have adequate coverage; check with your insurance agent or your company personnel department and save the $2 a day. On the other hand, if you are in an accident, know that the personal insurance will cover medical expenses, ambulance costs, etc., even if you receive insurance payments from other policies.

Gas Up!

Whatever you do, return your rental car to the agency with a full tank of gas. If you don't, the agency will gas it up at *their* pumps, at *their* price, and will add the charge to your rental bill. This is part of the deal, of course. You must pay for all gas used, and as the car was delivered to you with a full tank, you must return it with a full tank, or they'll fill it and charge you. The rip-off comes in the price they charge per gallon. While working on this book, I picked up my wife on her return from a business trip. We met at the rental car agency. She returned her rental car while I went to a neighboring gas station to fill up our family car. I paid $1.17 per gallon; her rental car was tanked up at $1.55 per gallon. And this was at one of the "budget" rental firms!

Whatever you do, return your rental car to the agency with a full tank of gas.

There are many other methods by which you can obtain the use of a car. Read on.

DRIVEAWAYS

In North America you can cut the costs of driving by signing up for a "driveaway," a private car entrusted by its owner to a firm which finds drivers to take the car to a certain destination. Often the car's owner is flying to his destination, but wants his car there as well. You must be over 21 (occasionally over 25), have a driver's license and references (easy to arrange). Foreign visitors need an International Drivers Permit. You call a driveaway firm after finding their number in the phone book or classified ad (usually under "Driveaways" or "Automobile Transport and Driveaway Companies"), ask if there is a car going to your destination, sign a contract, pay a deposit, and you're on your way with a full tank of gas. After that, fuel costs are usually your responsibility;

repairs are the owner's. On average you'll be expected to clock around 400 miles a day. You must deliver the car according to the schedule stated in the contract, although a phone call to the owner often yields concessions: "Alright, stop in New Orleans for a day. Enjoy yourself." By the way, AACON is one of the largest names to look for in the business.

PURCHASING A NEW OR USED CAR

If you've already been planning the purchase of a European car and, most important, if you'll be abroad for more than a month, you *may* (and this is a very iffy proposition) be able to save some money on purchasing a car for delivery overseas. Ten years ago, when the cost of shipping a car home was around $150, when taxes were low, and before European cars had to be specially manufactured to U.S. specifications for import to the U.S., the situation was favorable for buying a car in Europe, using it there, and then shipping it back. Now, particularly for the European small car, once you've factored in the additional charges for shipping (around $600), factory "prep" (say $200), U.S. import tax (about 2½%), your own local city and state taxes (8% or so), and possibly European delivery to the city of your choice (unless you're willing to go to the city where the factory is), you'll find that the only savings comes from your not having to rent a car. (In countries that levy a V.A.T., you will have to lay out that tax cost, although once the car has been exported (the law usually requires export within 6 months), you can apply for a full refund.

For expensive makes, of course, you would pay a higher rental fee and your savings on a purchase would be proportionately higher. Car dealers are chary of quoting prices by phone, and if you're considering overseas delivery of a *large luxury* car, person-to-person negotiation with the U.S. dealer should result in a savings of from 5% to 10% off the U.S. purchase price. So, even if your additional overseas costs (shipping, marine insurance, delivery, taxes, etc.) add up to $1000, depending on the price you'll stand a good chance of saving $500 to $1000 on the purchase price. This savings, plus the cost of renting a large car abroad (even for a month), would result in substantial dollar savings. (A BMW 730 would cost about $2500 a month, including insurance.) Don't forget to factor into your calculations the exchange rate of the dollar vis-à-vis the currency in which you pay for the car. A strong dollar, such as we have now as we go to press, makes additional savings possible.

Buying a Used Car

You're going to California for a month, and you'd like to have a car so you can get around L.A. Why not buy a used car, use it, and sell it at the end of the month? Of course, it's a gamble: how do I find a good car? What if it breaks down? How can I be sure I'll sell it again? Luck is involved, but with clear thinking and a bit of luck, it'll work out fine.

Consider this: used cars are priced according to year, mileage, and general condition. If you buy a used car for $500, put several thousand miles on it in a month or two, and don't get in any bad accidents, *the car has lost no value whatsoever!* You can sell it for what you paid, perhaps more. The year hasn't changed, the condition has not changed noticeably, and a few thousand miles more means nothing—it's the ten-thousands figure that counts. With luck and skill, you can have a car for a month for absolutely nothing; though in most cases you'll be out of pocket for gas, insurance, license and title fees, and sales tax.

HITCHHIKING AND RIDES

In many places, hitchhiking is the generally accepted means of transport. Sometimes the ride is understood to be free of charge, sometimes you will be expected to pay (perhaps the equivalent of bus fare), sometimes it is proper to offer payment, though the driver may refuse to accept it.

Don't dismiss hitching outright as antisocial and unsafe. Instead, ask around and get information on safety and local hitching customs. For example, in the U.S. there is no nationwide law against hitchhiking. Individual cities and states make their own laws. Almost anywhere, women must be much more careful than men. Also, be aware that "the thumb" is not a universally accepted signal that you want a ride. In many countries you are expected to flag down a vehicle with your hand, or wait at a gas station, roadside restaurant, or crossroads.

Pre-arranged rides, though usually more expensive than hitchhiking, are generally safer and more convenient. You can meet and talk with the driver and other passengers before you leave, and agree on sharing charges.

Rides are available almost everywhere, throughout the world, wherever travelers go. Bulletin boards in colleges, youth hostels, cafes, Y's, and inexpensive hotels are excellent places to search for the ride you want, or to post your own notice asking for riders to share expenses if you have the car. Some large American cities even have "ride centers," agents-for-profit who match up rides and riders for a small fee. For information leads, call the biggest college or university in the area. Many colleges operate formal ride services, and if they don't, they'll know who does.

9

Rail, Bus, and Other Cost-Effective Transportation

MAKING THE MOST OF TRAIN TRAVEL

Sometimes going by train is less expensive than going by other means, sometimes it's not. For a single person, the train is cheaper than going by car, more comfortable than going by bus, and sometimes more restful and convenient than going by plane.

Plane or Train?

Using the train to advantage takes careful thinking. As trains run from city center to city center, one doesn't pay for airport buses, downtown parking, and so forth. The fastest trains on some routes can rival the plane time, depending on the location of stations and airports. For instance, I used to take the night train between Istanbul and Ankara. I took a cheap public ferry to the station in Istanbul, got the train at 8 p.m., had a good dinner in the dining car, and went to bed in a private sleeping compartment at 11 p.m. At 6 a.m. the next morning I awoke to find the pastel colors of the Anatolian plateau rolling by my window. I washed and shaved in my compartment, wandered down to the dining car, finished breakfast as we entered the suburbs of Ankara, and alighted from the train at 7 a.m., fresh, shaved, breakfasted, and ready for the day.

To get right to the center of Ankara by 7 a.m. by plane, I would have had to go the night before; the alternative would be to have gotten up at 3 or 4 a.m. to get to the air terminal to catch the (expensive) airport bus so that I could catch the 6 a.m. flight. I'd touch down after 8:30 a.m., and by the time I was in the airport bus and headed into town it would be 9. The airport is 32 miles outside Ankara, and it would be 10 a.m. before I reached the center of the city. All this hassle cost twice as much as the train trip. The point is this: the plane trip took half the time, but not at the *right* time. And it cost double.

Using the train to best advantage is possible at home as well. Some routes are the ideal distance for a train trip: four hours or less for a daytime trip, eight hours or more for an overnight. When you compare the train with the plane, remember to add in all the costs of getting to and from the airport, plus the time this may take. We've all gone through that frustrating experience of spending three hours traveling to and from the airports for a 45-minute flight. By the way, in fog a 45-minute flight can turn into an all-day wait. Trains run in fog.

Overnighting on the Train

The same advantage is yours in other countries. Even if a sleeping compartment is very expensive (as in most of Europe), you can still get a decent night's sleep on a train. Underneath the seat cushion of every European compartment seat is a strap. Pull on that strap and your seat will "recline" just a bit; do the same thing to the strap under the seat across from yours, and you have a sort of bed. Pick an empty compartment if possible, and there is your "private" sleeping car.

The trick here is to choose a milk-run train, the slowest you can find. Often no one will be on it, you'll have plenty of time to sleep, and you will end up with a private or almost-private compartment.

To take the ultimate advantage of this form of accommodation, buy a Eurailpass before you leave home, and you can sleep on the train any night you choose. See Paris on Tuesday, and when you get tired, wander down to the Gare de Lyon and get the 9 p.m. to Marseilles. Have a night's rest, and awaken at 8:10 a.m. as the train pulls into Marseilles. Tour Marseilles on Wednesday, and at 10:53 p.m. catch the train back to Paris, arriving at 8:28 a.m. Thursday is thus another Paris day. It may be a bit disorienting, but you get your accommodation almost for free.

I say "almost," because the train back to Paris is an "all-couchette" train, on which you must pay a supplement for your couchette. The couchette is a shelf-like bed, somewhat more comfortable than pulling two seats together. You are given a pillow and perhaps a blanket of sorts.

European stations are marvels for the traveler who sleeps on trains. In France, Switzerland, and many other countries, major-city stations have private pay cubicles for washing up, shaving, even bathing. Rental electric razors—sterilized automatically between uses—hang on the wall, and buzz into action when you drop a coin in the slot. After a shave, drop in another coin and get a spritz of cologne! Vending machines sell toothbrushes and paste, soap, moist towelettes, combs, and shoe polish. You may even find a very simple lodging with cot-equipped cubicles so you can have a snooze, or even a full night's rest.

Discount Fares and Special Deals

Every railroad has special, discounted fares for certain classes of passengers. Children, senior citizens, families traveling together, military personnel in uniform, students—in a few countries the list is even longer. But even if you don't fit one of these categories, you may be able to save money.

Often during the "off-season" you'll find all kinds of specials available. During 1981–82 for instance, from November to April, Amtrak was offering a special "Circle the West" ticket, (Los Angeles-LasVegas-Seattle-Chicago-San Antonio-Los Angeles) that discounted the regular fare by 32%. In the East you could circle from New York via Montreal, Ottawa, Toronto, Niagara Falls, and New York for $108. Watch out for these good values.

EURAILPASS: Undoubtedly one of the best bargains in rail travel, the Eurailpass is superb if you intend to crisscross the continent for an extended time.

This pass is good for *unlimited* first-class rail travel throughout all of Europe (other than the British Isles) for a specified amount of time. As we go to press, a 15-day pass costs $250; 21-day pass, $320; one-month, $390; a two-month, $530; and a three-month, $650. The best value goes to the traveler on a two-month vacation or longer. Anyone under the age of 26 can purchase a Eurail Youthpass, entitling them to unlimited second-class transportation for two months for only $350.

In some cases the Eurailpass is good also on lake steamers and ferries. Always inquire—the answer can only be "No." You must purchase the ticket outside

Europe. Write or visit the nearest European railway office in any major city in North America or see a travel agent.

OTHER CONTINENTAL PASSES: Similar continental passes are offered to foreign visitors in the United States by Amtrak. The USA Railpass is sold only outside North America to non-residents of the U. S. and Canada. It's good for unlimited rail travel on all Amtrak lines, but does not include sleeping car accommodations. A traveler must begin using it 90 days after it's issued.

THE NATIONAL PASSES: Most countries throughout the world sell special passes for travel throughout their railroad networks. These can represent huge savings. Some of them also give you other advantages. For example, the French National Railroads France Vacances pass throws in a one-day car rental, a four-day Parisian Metro pass, round-trip transportation between airport and air terminal in Paris, and a museum pass. There are also special reductions for families and senior citizens. A similar unlimited mileage Britrail Pass is available for travel throughout England, Scotland, and Wales. It must be purchased outside Britain. The Swiss railways offer some excellent deals. Some countries offer special coupons that reflect discounts. Find out about them from the Tourist Offices *before you leave*.

Rail Packages

Look into these. In many countries it is possible to buy a package tour of transportation-and-hotel based on a train ticket and a budget lodging. Since the tour company is not chartering one particular vehicle (as with airplanes), but rather is utilizing a continuous system (the railroads and ferries), you can often set your own departure and return dates. Once I bought a "tour" from London to Paris and back which gave me reduced-price train and ferry tickets, three nights at a budget hotel in Paris, and I was allowed to "break" my tour for a four-day side trip to Geneva after I had stayed the three nights in Paris. I tailored the trip exactly to my needs, and got it at a discount price. If I subtracted the normal train fares from the tour price, the hotel in Paris ended up costing about $3 per night.

More and more railroads are operating their own tour agencies, putting together such packages in conjunction with hotels, resorts, and rental car agencies, in order to entice you into taking the train. Even if you can't speak the language, write down your itinerary, look up the word for "tour," "package," or "discount trip," and present the paper to a travel agent or railroad clerk.

In North America, Amtrak and VIA Rail Canada operate many tours (Amtrak runs close to 200) of all kinds. Although railfare is often additional, the accommodations packages can be great bargains and other special arrangements such as car rental discounts may also be available. For information write to Amtrak, 400 North Capitol St. NW, Washington, DC 20001 (tel. 202/383-3850).

Do-It-Yourself Tours

Remember that on most rail journeys, you can hop off and on trains at will, breaking your trip whenever and wherever you like. So if you plan to see Europe from London to Vienna, buy a round-trip ticket London-Vienna-London, and stop in Brussels, Cologne, Bonn, Frankfurt, and Linz along the way. A distinct bonus of rail over air travel.

City and Commuter Train Travel

On heavily traveled commuter lines, which include some intercity ones, you can save money by riding when the crush of commuters doesn't—which is exactly what you want to do in any case. Ask about "peak" and "off-peak," or similarly named fares. If you make a round trip in a day, or within a certain number of days, you may get a discount.

Always ask about special discounted ticket booklets for subways, metros, undergrounds, etc.

Special Hints on Riding the European Rails

European trains are of two kinds: magnificent and awful. The magnificents provide superb, rapid service and can be recognized by the fact that they carry names as well as numbers—the famous *Simplon-Orient Express* and the *Golden Arrow,* for instance. They normally run overnight, stop only in the largest cities, and cut hours from your travel time. Thus the Intercity Express makes the trip from Munich to Frankfurt in 3 hours and 45 minutes. A lesser train traveling exactly the same route takes two hours longer. If you always schedule your trips and your connections for the sleek named-trains, traveling in Europe can be a cinch.

On these named expresses, you will also quickly learn that you can pay as much as 33% to 50% more for the privilege of riding first class and getting an inch or two of extra seat padding. It follows that you should always travel second-class on a major European express; a second-class ticket will purchase a perfectly comfortable, well-padded seat. Second-class should be trusted only on the expresses though; elsewhere you could find yourself sitting on a very uncomfortable wooden bench in a veritable rattletrap. By sticking to second-class on the expresses, train transportation costs become very reasonable. For example, the trip from Florence to Rome costs only $12.40; from Barcelona to Paris it's only $79.

SCHEDULES: If you are planning a grand rail tour of Europe including Britain, you might want to get hold of the latest copy of the Thomas Cook Continental Timetable of European railroads. This comprehensive 500+ page timetable details all of Europe's main line rail services with great accuracy. It is available exclusively in North America from Forsyth Travel Library, P. O. Box 2975, Shawnee Mission, KS 66201, at a cost of $15.95 including postage.

GOING BY BUS

Buses go everywhere. The modern emphasis on good roads has fostered spiderwebs of bus routes in virtually every country.

All else being equal, bus travel is not the most preferable way to go. Seats are cramped, conveniences are limited; you may have to put up with music, excessive heating or air conditioning. On trains you may have a café or restaurant, and you can walk around; train seats are larger and roomier than bus seats. But generally the train costs 20% more than the bus, travels more slowly, and may not go where you want to go.

Special Passes

You can save money on bus tickets by asking about tour or excursion prices, round-trip or frequent-user discounts, or unlimited-mileage passes. The unlimited-mileage passes often come in several fashions, and you may qualify for extra discounts if you're a foreign tourist and purchase the tickets outside the country in which you will use them.

Most famous of the United States passes is the Trailways U.S.A. Pass, also called the Eagle Pass. This is currently available to foreign *and* U.S.

residents—providing unlimited mileage privileges for 7-, 15-, and 30-day periods at low costs. An additional bonus lies in the fact that the passes can be extended for another 10 days for only $10 a day (in early 1982 at least).

There's no doubt about it—bus travel can be extremely cheap. In some countries the buses have even begun competing with the airlines by offering ludicrously low fares. At one time last year in England, you could go from London to Birmingham for the ridiculous sum of $5. Keep your eyes and ears open.

Europe's Magic Bus

A low-cost alternative for long- or short-distance transportation around Europe is the private bus line. One of the most dependable is Magic Bus, with offices in Los Angeles (15600 Roscoe Blvd., Van Nuys, CA 91406; tel. 213/994-0329), London (the main office, at 67-69 New Oxford St., WC 1; tel. 836-7799), Paris, Athens, Barcelona, and Munich. The fares are low: London to Amsterdam is £13 (about $26) one way, £25 round trip: Paris to Athens costs 350 francs (at the current rate of 6 francs to the dollar, a mere $58) one way, 550 francs round trip. You can book in advance, always advisable in the summer season. At this writing, Magic Bus is planning a New York-Los Angeles-San Francisco route to begin operation in summer 1982.

The United States' Alternative Buses

In America **Grey Rabbit** runs low-cost buses from coast to coast in three to four days. The fare from New York to California is $109. Stops are possible in between—the itinerary and route are left up to the driver and at times there are side trips to the Grand Canyon, Saratoga Hot Springs, etc. Buses are equipped with mattresses. For details, contact New York Ride Center, 134 W. 32 St., New York, NY 10001 (tel. 212/279-3870, or in San Francisco, 415/524-5404).

Another similar operation is the **Green Tortoise,** which connects San Francisco and Los Angeles, Boston and New York. It goes to New Orleans every year from San Francisco, Boston, and New York, and during Mardi Gras the camper buses remain in the French Quarter for two weeks in order to provide accommodations and sanitary facilities. The Green Tortoise also travels from the West Coast to Alaska, Baja California, and Mexico. At press time, a one-way, cross-country trip of seven to ten days was $199; the four-week Alaska trip was $499. For information, write to the Green Tortoise, P.O. Box 24459, San Francisco, CA 94124; or call: in Boston, 617/265-8533; in New York, 212/431-3348; and in San Francisco, 415/386-1798.

Bus Packages

From "The Historic East" to the "Old West Heritage," there is a bus package tour to suit almost every taste—and size of pocketbook. If you think you'd like to take a bus tour, it will pay to shop around for the best value. Here are some of the questions to keep in mind when choosing a bus package tour: Do you know exactly what services (meals, accommodations, etc.) are included in the tour price? Does the tour offer special features you'd be able to take advantage of? For example, can you join the tour later, or leave it earlier and get a refund for the unused portion of the trip? How large a group does the tour include? Is there enough free time for you to do some exploring on your own, or is the tour overly regimented for your taste? Is smoking permitted in the motorcoach? Is the tour operator a member of the U.S. Tour Operators Association? USTOA members must carry liability insurance covering their tours and must maintain a bond or other security to reimburse purchasers or depositors in case of the member's bankruptcy or insolvency.

"The Historic East," by the way, is a Globus-Gateway trip; it costs $538 and visits New York, Philadelphia, Gettysburg, Williamsburg, Washington, D.C., and other historic sites. "Old West Heritage," offered by Four Winds Tours, is a 15-day, $1468 tour; it includes Yellowstone, the Grand Tetons, and Mount Rushmore.

Jitney Cabs

A jitney cab is a taxi shared by several travelers who may not know one another but who band together and split the cost of a given trip. The taxi may be an ancient Chrysler limousine, a shiny new seven-passenger Mercedes, a minibus, or just a car. The ride may be from First Street to Fifth Street, from downtown to the suburbs, from city to city, or even country to country.

Jitney cabs can afford to run where buses can't, for a jitney can run profitably on a handful of people where a bus would need several dozen. Jitneys are almost always faster than buses, more direct, and often more comfortable. They usually cost a bit more than the bus.

In the Middle East, jitneys are especially popular. Called *dolmush* (Turkey), *sherut* (Israel), *servis* (Lebanon and other Arab countries), they are operated by hundreds of little private agencies, and they travel virtually everywhere, even to and from Europe!

In Mexico, they're called *peseros*; look for jitneys in many other countries. Hotel clerks know what they are (if they exist), who runs them, and which agencies operate to which destinations. Often, a jitney heading out on a long trip will be willing to swing by your hotel and pick you up.

Jitney drivers in foreign countries may try to rip you off on the fare. Confirm the fare with a hotel clerk, policeman, or ideally with several other passengers.

BY MOTORCYCLE, MOPED, BICYCLE

You can rent, lease, or buy a two-wheeled conveyance if you use some ingenuity. Al fresco travel has its own rewards and drawbacks, however. It is cheaper than a car, more fun and adventurous at times. But it is also exhausting, wet, hot in the sun, uncomfortable, and more dangerous. Theft is more of a problem, theft of your things, your vehicle, or parts of your vehicle. Before you take off on a long motorcycle trip, read *Jupiter's Travels,* by Ted Simon (Garden City, NY: Doubleday & Company, 1980). The author rode a motorcycle around the world, encountered every possible delight and dilemma, and arrived at the end of the journey a different person.

Traveling by bicycle shares some of the characteristics of motorcycle travel, but over long distances cyclists usually travel in groups on organized tours, which is safer, more convenient, and more fun. Guidebooks to bicycle trips abound on bookstore shelves, and several organizations sponsor bicycle trips in various parts of the world.

Bicycles and mopeds are, of course, ideal for hopping around cities and can be rented very cheaply. Depending on the size and power a moped can get as many as 150 miles to the gallon. For this energy-saving wonder you'll pay, let's say in London, $10 a day, $49 a week, and $90 a month plus insurance and VAT.

GOING BY SHIP

So much for the major forms of transportation. We come now to the subject of sea transportation. If you're looking for a cost-effective way of getting to a particular destination (cruises are another matter) then you're not going to find it on the high seas. Even before the fuel crisis, shipline after shipline announced that they were ceasing to operate particular vessels, and the process has continued. The New York Harbor piers are eerily quiet these days. Some attempts have been made to encourage folk to travel by sea, but they're few and far between. For example, British Airways has a special arrangement with Cunard whereby you can fly one way and return aboard the *Queen Elizabeth II* or vice versa. Costs are still extremely high (for the summer of 1982, rates are from $1260 to $5430 per person round trip), although many people still say that you should experience such a crossing at least once in a lifetime.

Freighters

For the most part, you can forget about these too. With the exception of occasional ships leaving from Norfolk or Newport News, Virginia, the average freighter charges very little less than the average passenger liner. And even if you save some money, you'll nearly double your travel time (most freighters take from eight to ten days to cross the Atlantic) and you'll place yourself at the mercy of erratic and sporadic sailing schedules (some passengers wait a week in New York for their freighter to finally leave).

This is not to say that freighter travel isn't a unique and satisfying experience.

For information about freighter travel write to the following organizations:

Travltips Freighter Travel Association, 163-09TS Depot Rd., Flushing, NY 11358 (tel. 212/939-2400); **Ford's Freighter Travel Guide,** P.O. Box 505, Woodland Hills, CA 91365 (tel. 213/347-1677); **Pearl's Freighter Trips,** 175 Great Neck Rd., Suite 3061, Great Neck, NY 11021 (tel. 516/487-8351).

PART THREE

Saving Money
on the Trip

10

Beating the High Price of Hotels

All you want to do is wash, change, sleep, wash, dress, and depart. Why, in some cities of the world today, does this simple human process cost you $100 to $200? Simple: because the establishments charging these prices are not principally interested in giving you a place to wash, dress, and sleep. They are designed so you can swim, dine, chatter in magnificent lobbies and public rooms, pursue a romance, clinch a business deal, have drinks or breakfast brought to your bed, send a Telex message, get your clothes cleaned, park a car, hold a wedding reception. You are not paying merely to sleep, you are paying for the right or *potential* right to do all of these various things.

HOW IT ALL BEGAN

Centuries ago, hostelries were for sleeping. The English word *inn* is over a thousand years old. At first it meant just *house,* abode, lodging—a place to come in from the elements and rest. By the year 1400, an inn was also a place where travelers could put up for the night and get something to eat. An inn fulfilled the traveler's basic needs. If there were no inn, the traveler would have to ask at a house for hospitality. By the early 1800s, inns were coming to be known as taverns. The interesting people who passed through town often put up at the local inn, and any local person bored with hometown life could drop by the inn and find out about the rest of the country or the rest of the world over a hot meal or a cold drink.

The "public house," that is, the house built for anyone to use, was becoming a social center along with the church and the manor. It had already— several centuries ago—strayed from its role as a provider of the bare essentials for travelers.

About this time the *hotel* appeared on the scene. Borrowed from French, *hotel* had originally been *hostel,* the French equivalent of the English inn. But by the late 1700s and early 1800s, a *hotel* in French was a grand and imposing building, a rich man's city mansion or the city hall. Taken into English, it signified a large and particularly sumptuous inn.

In 1766, one English traveler by the name of Smollett was already exclaiming, "The expence of living at an hotel is enormous!" Another traveler mocked the pretentiousness of the word: "Groping your way to the inn—I beg pardon—*hotel*. . . ." This progress from simple lodging to sumptuous luxury is still going on.

From its beginning as a social center, the hotel has advanced to become a temporary office and corporate headquarters, housing for a convention (the modern equivalent of a tradesmen's fair), and quarters for mass travel—what in medieval or Renaissance times would have been a festival. It has little to do with mere washing, changing, and sleeping any more, except that all of us have to do that on a daily basis to remain healthy and happy.

Luckily for us all, the urge to travel and the basic needs have not changed—and the means to fulfill them are still at hand. You can still knock on the door of a private home and find clean lodgings for the night; you can still come across simple, basic accommodations for which an honest price is charged, and which will not leave you exclaiming, like Smollett, "The expence of living at an hotel is enormous!" This applies to every single country in the world.

Later in this chapter I'll discuss the various kinds of inexpensive lodgings available and how and where you can find them, but first here are some tips on how you can enjoy the wonderful facilities of the luxury hotel or resort at bargain prices.

GETTING VALUE AT FULL-FACILITY HOTELS

Wherever you stay, you should understand how these establishments put prices on their rooms, and how you can get the lowest possible prices.

The leading fiction among travelers is that hotels have set prices for their rooms. Sure, there are the so-called "rack rates," the prices printed up in brochures and charged to the unsuspecting traveler who comes in off the street and says, "I want a room." But in fact, hotel managers are working in a volatile marketplace which resembles nothing so much as an Oriental bazaar. A big festival or event will fill the city and all its hotels with visitors, and the managers can charge the high "rack rates," plus perhaps a "special supplement," plus a hefty service charge. However, when off-season comes, the weather is unpleasant, and there's nothing going on, hotels will rent out rooms for next to nothing.

How do you get special prices for rooms? You follow these procedures:

Look for special offers and plan far enough ahead to take advantage of them, or bargain on the spot for a room.

Weekend Packages

As with car rentals, hotel discounts and special offers coincide with the weekly and the yearly business cycle. For example, during the week, city hotels are fully occupied with out-of-town businesspeople. When they go home at weekends the rooms are empty, and to fill the gap between Thursday and Monday most major hotels offer weekend packages, which are one of the best bargains around.

All you want to do is wash, change, sleep, wash, dress, and depart. Why, in some cities of the world today, does this simple human process cost you $100 to $200?

Here are three examples among the many New York hotels that offer reduced-rate weekend packages. At the U.N. Plaza (1 U.N. Plaza on E. 44th St., New York, NY 10017; tel. 212/355-3400 or 800/228-9000), a striking glass-sheathed highrise that bills itself as a resort in the sky, the special "Weekend over New York" cost $42.50 per person per night, double occupancy, including full American breakfast, free parking, and use of the pool, sauna, and exercise room. Regular doubles cost from $135 to $160 a night.

In the heart of midtown Manhattan (Park Avenue at Grand Central), you can stay at the Grand Hyatt for two nights (Friday and Saturday) for $39 per person per night on their "Live and Love New York Weekend." Regular doubles are $135 a night. Call 800/228-9000 (in New York City, 883-1234) for details. To attract weekenders, one of the city's newest hotels, Vista International, at the World Trade Center (tel. 212/938-9100), has a "Happy & Healthy" package— $99 per person, double occupancy, two nights. Price includes use of their fitness center (pool, exercise machines, racquetball court), a health lunch, transportation to midtown, and parking. Standard doubles are usually $130 per night.

How do you find out about such packages? Write or call the appropriate Convention and Tourist Bureau and ask them. In New York, for example, the Convention and Tourist Bureau will send you a free brochure listing all the weekend and other packages offered by the major hotels. If you already have a destination chosen and a hotel picked out, call the hotel and ask what they have available.

By the way, at resorts you'll often find the reverse is true. For example, during the winter ski resorts fill up on weekends with skiing fanatics, so you'll find resorts offering special reduced midweek packages including reduced lift tickets, etc.

Off-Season Discounts

On a yearly cycle, you'll find hotels and resorts offering fantastic bargains during their off-season. Off-season varies according to your destination. Here are the dates that airlines consider low season for ten European countries: September 15 to May 14 for Austria, England, France, Italy, Spain, Sweden, and Yugoslavia; from September 15 to May 30 for Czechoslovakia; from September 1 to May 14 for Ireland; and from November 1 to March 31 for Portugal.

If you choose to go just at the end of the on-season or just before it begins, you can enjoy everything the destination has to offer at a substantial reduction in price.

The super-luxurious Little Dix Bay resort hotel on Virgin Gorda island in the Caribbean offers a telling example: You can enjoy the quiet elegance of this Rockresort from November 1 through December 19 at $180 daily for a single, $200 double, including three meals daily. The very next day, December 20, until mid-May, the cost escalates to $265 in a single, $285 daily for two persons. What a difference a day makes! Summer rates are even cheaper: $160 daily single, $180 double—all for the same deluxe services that cost so much more in season.

Again, last winter British Airways was offering standby passengers rooms at first-class Grand Metropolitan Hotels in London for $22 per person double occupancy—rooms that generally cost up to $140 a night in season!

Package Tours

This is yet another way of enjoying a full-facility establishment at a substantially discounted rate. In fact these tours are a boon to the traveler who has a limited amount of vacation time.

The tour packager relies on volume to obtain massive discounts off hotel accommodation prices. On any tour you will most likely have the choice of several hotels ranging from standard to deluxe. For the deluxe accommodations you'll pay a supplement, but you'll still be staying at the hotel at a rate that you could never command as an independent traveler unless you were taking advantage of the weekend package or something similar.

If you do choose to take a package, check that the tour operator is a member of the U. S. Tour Operators Association before you make your reservation, and ask your friends and acquaintances if they have ever traveled with the company. Note their opinions and experiences. Also, you may want to check with the Better Business Bureau about the company's complaint record. Then read the brochures very carefully.

Look at what you get on your tour for the price. What you actually get and what it may seem to say that you get may be two very different things. Be alert.

Even after all these caveats, on a one-week or two-week vacation you'll rarely beat the value, whether you go to Austria on a ski package or to Mexico or the Caribbean on a sun package. You might say the package tour is our somewhat telescoped modern version of the Grand Tour.

Bargaining on Arrival

To accomplish getting a room for less on arrival, you'll need to do two things. First, find out the state of the market. Ask about occupancy rates, directly or indirectly, to people who would know. To an airlines clerk, "Things pretty busy in Boston these days, lots of visitors?" To a tourist information officer, "It should be pretty easy to find a room in San Francisco these days, no?" To a taxi driver, "What's the hotel situation like—lots of empty rooms?" To the front-desk clerk at a hotel, "You seem pretty busy; anyplace around here with lots of empty rooms?" Finding out the state of the market takes only a few minutes and a few well-placed questions. Second, read the following tips on bargaining techniques.

BARGAINING ETIQUETTE: Remember to look for the Point of Mutual Advantage: you've determined that the hotel situation is not tight, and that hotels are actively encouraging people to stay at cut rates (week-end package offerings are useful indicators).

The only remaining hurdle is one of etiquette. The secret is this: let the hotel do you a favor. Don't browbeat a desk clerk by saying "Look, I know this place is empty as a tomb. You should give me a room for a buck!" Instead, use one of these approaches:

Ask if there is a "commercial rate." Some hotels

offer lower rates to frequent business travelers. The Point of Mutual Adventage is that the hotel gets the traveler's business time after time, and the traveler gets it a bit cheaper each time. But in the industry, "commercial rate" is also a buzzword for discount. It saves face for the hotel, it lets the hotel do you a favor. They don't have to admit they're empty-ish, the ultimate shame in the hotel industry (success is measured not just in profits, but in high occupancy rates). They fill a room, and make some money. You save.

The best time to bargain for a room is late in the day, when the clerk knows for sure that he's going to have empty rooms that night.

If the "commercial rate" doesn't work, or if the price quoted is still too high, use this tack: "I was looking for a room at $30, and wondered if you had anything in that range." If your price is simply too far below the hotel's dignity, the clerk will say "No, we have nothing in that range." You can now raise your offer, or you can ask if the clerk knows of any hotel nearby which might have prices in that range, or which might be fairly empty. (The clerk won't mind telling you, with a gloating look in his eye, that the Fleabag Arms down the street is only 40% booked!) Besides garnering valuable information, your question lets the clerk know that you're willing to take your light shoulder bag and walk out the door with your money.

The best time to bargain for a room is late in the day, when the clerk knows for sure that he's going to have empty rooms that night. He knows that if the room isn't sold for something, its value as a place to stay for that particular night is gone forever. Suppertime, the customary time to which reservations are held, is late enough, though later is better. At 11 p.m., boy, do you have bargaining power! And if the city is not booked solid, you'll find a room at a price that's good. Don't worry.

OTHER THINGS TO BARGAIN FOR: Simple price bargaining is not the only fertile field for savings. If you are creative, you can save a bundle even when the hotel's dignity or the clerk's unwillingness to go through the registration procedure will not allow a substantial rate discount. Look at these bargaining points:

● Get two rooms for the (full) price of one.

● Get a suite for the full price of a standard room.

● Get a 5% discount for paying in cash (you save the hotel from paying that much to the credit card company).

● Get permission for extra people to share a double room for no extra charge.

● Get extra nights for free. Tell them you'll pay for two nights at full price, but you want a third night free. What do they have to lose?

● Get big discounts for longer stays. Even if you've got a discount for tonight's lodging, ask for more if you plan to stay a while.

In bargaining for discounts, you must concentrate on getting for yourself those things which cost the hotel little or nothing. Don't try to get meals, as foodstuffs not sold today can be refrierated and sold tomorrow. But don't pay for things such as tennis court use, which in busy times are subject to a fee; or parking, when it will cost the hotel nothing to keep your car in an empty underground lot.

Note that these discount strategies can be used at

any hotel, but are most successful at the huge, expensive, multi-service places. In effect, what you're doing is bringing these convention palaces back down to charging prices only for shelter, bed, and privacy. If that's all they can get, they'll gladly take it. And don't look at bargaining in an expensive hotel as a way to get budget accommodations. You'll never turn a Hilton into a tourist home. Rather, you get excellent value-for-money: for a moderate price you get luxury accoutrements such as the downtown location, the indoor pool, the panoramic view, the air conditioning, and covered parking.

ONE LAST ENCOURAGEMENT: Don't take no for an answer until you're certain the answer is no. You can't browbeat a hotel clerk into meeting your price, but you can push that person to the point of asking himself, "Can I really not sell the room for $30? The boss said $40, but I can get rid of this persistent person with the shoulder bag and get back to my mystery novel if I rent a room on the back side of the hotel for $35. The boss won't quibble."

THE CHEAPEST HOTEL AND MOTEL ROOMS

In North American cities, the place to look for an inexpensive room is most often in a motel on the outskirts. In many (but not all) cases, this means you must have a car, because public transport to the center is either slow, or infrequent, or nonexistent.

Downtown hotels have largely become the preserve of expense-account travelers, conventioneers, and the wealthy. Of course, the convenience of staying right downtown is apparent: you get more time to see the sights as they're right outside, you needn't worry about traffic jams, or parking (after that first time when you arrive), you can head back to your room for a forgotten guidebook or a quick nap very easily. With a motel on the outskirts, about the only advantage is price. But with the average double room in a decent downtown hotel costing $70 to $100 per night, a motel room at $30 to $45 looks very good indeed—you can stay twice as long for the same price.

Here are some tips:

- Look for "clusters" of motels, often near major highway intersections; if one or two are full, or expensive, you can check others nearby.

- Figure your commuting costs into the motel price when comparing that price with a downtown hotel's; if you must drive ten miles, cross a toll bridge, and park in a pay lot, this may add substantially to the cost of your motel stay.

Budget Motel Chains

Anyone who drives the major highways of North America is familiar with the budget chains, motels set up to undercut the high prices of such fancy places as the Holiday Inns. How do they do it? First, they build on cheap land; then, they use very cost-efficient construction techniques. Finally, the facilities are comfortable and quite adequate, but there are few extras: no meeting rooms, audio-visual equipment, grand lobbies, restaurants, or bars.

Though you can usually find the budget motels by following their billboards on the highways, it helps immensely to have the budget chains' directories in the glove compartment of your car. You can get the directories for the price of several postcards. If you contemplate any sort of long-distance travel in North America, buy 14 postcards the next time you're at the post office, write "Please send me a copy of your motel directory," and your name and address on the back, and then address the cards to the firms listed in

Appendix 3. In a few days the free directories will start to arrive. After two weeks, you'll have a full set. Put a rubber band around them, stuff them in the glove compartment, and you'll be equipped with a free, do-it-yourself, up-to-the-minute guidebook of budget motels in North America.

SPECIAL INEXPENSIVE LODGINGS

Now let's turn to the inexpensive lodgings that I was talking about in the introduction to this chapter. How can you find these inexpensive lodgings? Specific information is helpful, because even from earliest times, one house or another in a village or town was usually designated as the inn or hospitality house. (Perhaps it had an extra room, or its occupants wanted to earn a bit of money in exchange for the service.) But much more important than specific directions or recommendations is an *awareness* of how lodging places operate, and why.

When you see a roadside guest house, don't succumb to that weird twentieth-century trauma by which normal people are filled with terror, their courage flees them when confronted by the prospect of an unstandardized product.

The basic difference between an old-style inn and a new-style inn and a new-style hotel is this: the inn was a building which *came to be used* as a lodging for travelers, whereas the hotel was a building that was *designed to be used* by travelers. Therefore, the hotel was—from the very beginning—supposed to be a very profitable business enterprise. It was designed and built to accommodate and to please those who would and could pay more.

This ancient difference is still evident today. A Hilton or Sheraton was *built* for the business traveler. A guest house, tourist home, bed-and-breakfast, or dormitory was *built to do something else:* house a family, or students at school. Only *incidentally* is it a lodging for travelers, and therein lies the difference. It is not equipped with all of the luxury facilities that are designed and built into a hotel; it would be very expensive to convert it; and the proprietors are not interested in converting it into luxury accommodations.

Many variations on these themes exist, and in fact some inns have become exclusive, expensive, and overly fancy, while some hotels and motels may offer very good rates. But in general, you can save money by directing your efforts to finding accommodations in a building that was not built primarily to house travelers.

A Room in a Private Home

You can find these virtually everywhere, because the urge to take in travelers and earn a little extra money from surplus space is universal. In the U.S., "tourist homes" were the places our thrifty grandparents and great-grandparents stayed when they had no friends or relatives in town. Many of today's American tourist homes, guest houses and bed-and-breakfast places survive from that time, and show their Victorian-era origins.

You've passed them on the road and along the main street in a small town: signs that say "Guests," or "Overnight Guests," or "Murphy's Tourist Home." With the advent of the modern motel and the ulcer-making schedule, most travelers did just that—pass these places by in favor of standardized accommodations where they could just pull off the highway at any time of the day or night, without reservations, and find a private room with bath and toilet. No lady of the house to get out of bed if you arrived at midnight, no walking down the hall to the bathroom, no questions asked, no pleasantries to make, no proprieties— except payment—to be observed. No surprises, no variety, no human contact, please! I've got miles to cover.

How do you tell a good guest house or tourist home from a bad one? You look at it . . . and no self-respecting guest house owner will ever refuse to show you the room. (If they do, there's something wrong with the room, the owner, or the house.)

Some guest houses closed down when business slowed down; others closed for another reason: crime. By car, strangers could come from far or near, and the more people who had cars, the more chance that one or two of them might steal something or cause trouble.

Surprisingly, many guest houses didn't close, but have continued in operation through the "motel decades," and they continue today. Travel through any small New England town and you're sure to spot one or two guest houses. While the fancy "country inn" a block away is charging $95 per night for hyped-up "charm" and "atmosphere," the lady who runs the guest house will ask $14 for two, and will offer authentic warmth in the bargain.

How do you locate a good guest house or tourist home? By asking at a local chamber of commerce, tourist information booth or room-finding service. The latter are very popular in European towns and cities (often located in central train stations) where hundreds of rooms in dozens of houses can benefit from a central clearing office for room requests. In small resort towns throughout the world, people with rooms to rent for the night, for the week, or longer, will meet incoming trains, buses, and ferry boats (Greek islands, for example). They may have a handful of cards printed with the name, phone number, address, and directions to the house; or they may just ask, "Need a room?"

Or you may simply drive past a tourist home in a small town that displays a sign out front. *Stop your car and look!* Don't succumb to that weird twentieth-century trauma by which normal people are filled with terror, their courage flees them, when confronted by the prospect of an unstandardized product. As for dealing with the guest house or tourist home owner, that person is in the lodging business just like the hotelier and motel owner, but on a more modest scale.

How do you tell a good guest house or tourist home from a bad one? You look at it. As it is not a standardized product, you're not expected to register and pay up until you've inspected the facilities—the owner will *expect* that you want to examine the room, the beds, the bath—and learn the price. This only takes a few minutes, and no self-respecting guest house owner will ever refuse to show you the room. (If they do, there's something wrong with the room, the owner, or the house.) If you decide to take the room—fine. If you don't take it, the owner will figure it's not what you wanted, and he'll wait for the next ring. As for you, head down the road and perhaps the next tourist home will have that double bed, or garden view, or extra cot for the baby that you'd really like to have.

The Bed-and-Breakfast Movement in North America

In recent years, North Americans have been opening their homes to travelers. The increase in hotel prices, and a new familiarity with lodgings in the rest of the world, have led many people to consider renting rooms to travelers. The modern tactic for making it work in huge, modern cities where crime from transients is a problem is the bed-and-breakfast association. These private clearinghouses take reservations, set rates, provide directions, and weed out the undesirables. Bed-and-breakfast associations have sprung up in every major American city recently, and more are being organized every day. Entrepreneurs are compiling nationwide lists of bed-and-breakfasts leagues, and travel writers are producing guidebooks which deal exclusively with bed-and-breakfasts, or which include information about certain houses and leagues.

Specific addresses and tips are given in Appendix 2. But in any city, a riffle throught the phone book (stopping at logical places: "Bed and Breakfast," "Guest House Accommodation," "Lodging Bureau") will often produce the desired number. If not, a call to the Tourist Bureau or Convention and Visitors' Bureau (every city of any size has one of these, under a similar name) will get you the information you want.

What about accommodations? What's the room like? The officer at the bed-and-breakfast association will describe a room or rooms to you, tell you about its location, and quote the price. Associations try to aim for a fairly high standard: private bath, television, air conditioning, etc. But any room that is neat and reasonably commodious is usually accepted for booking, and the traveler pays only for what he gets. A plainish room comes at a lower price. With the room comes a fairly full breakfast, perhaps not bacon-eggs-cereal-home-fries-juice-porridge, but more than just rolls and coffee. You can find out about the breakfast when you find out about the room that goes with it. After you've sampled it, you can register compliments or complaints with the association, too. Most B&B's would much rather have their association receive the former than the latter.

Pensions and Other Special Accommodations

Besides tourist homes and bed-and-breakfasts, many other types of accommodation provide the simple, traditional services of the age-old inn at lower rates than the large luxury modern hotels.

In many European countries, some families do more than take in transient visitors and give them breakfast—they feed them as well. The classic *pension* (French) or *pensione* (Italy) is one or more large apartments with several rooms let to guests by the week or month. Meals are family-style, and are included with the room in the weekly price. Sometimes you can make arrangements for breakfast and dinner only, at a slightly lower price. This is probably what you want, as you will want to try some restaurants, and you won't want to traipse all the way back to your pension every day for lunch.

If you choose to go just at the end of the on-season or just before it begins, you can enjoy everything the destination has to offer at a substantial reduction in price.

How do you locate a pension? Through a lodging service such as exists in many cities, through a guidebook, or through another pension. If you have the name of one pension, you can find all the others. Pension owners keep track of one another.

Different countries have different types of moderately priced accommodations where travelers have been lodging down through the centuries. In England and Switzerland, you'll find small country inns as well as bed-and-breakfast places and pensions; in Denmark they're called *kros* while in Japan they're known as *minshuku* (private homes) or *ryokans* (moderately priced inns). In Spain the *paradores* are a good value; in Portugal the *estalagems* and *pensãos* are similar.

Ask the tourist offices about such accommodations. Not only will you get good value for money, you'll also really savor the local flavor.

LESS ORTHODOX ACCOMMODATIONS

For trips of a different nature, one can take advantage of various less orthodox accommodations. Because of the splendid benefits in some of these plans, you may just want to alter your travel plans and make them fit the accommodations, rather than vice-versa.

Home-Swapping and Time-Sharing

Home-swapping and time-sharing are twin concepts with many of the same benefits and disadvantages. Both of them involve a hefty commitment: you've got to be willing to let someone live in your home with your things while you're away, or you've got to be willing to pay a substantial sum for the right to share a place and its furnishings with others. If you are willing to do these things, read on.

Both home-swapping and time-sharing have a crucial element: location. If you live in Timbuktu, it's going to be very difficult to find someone who wants to swap homes with you. With an apartment in Manhattan or San Francisco, you can write your home-swapping ticket anywhere in the world, however. The same goes for time-sharing. If you buy one or two weeks in a condominium at Lake Mudbath, you can expect to swap only with those who have time-sharing condos in Blackfly Woods or Revolting Sands, whereas a week's time-sharing rights in Acapulco or

Vail will open the door to a swap anywhere you like. *Someone has got to want your place before any sort of a swap will work.*

A Hilton or Sheraton was *built* for the business traveler. A guest house, tourist home, bed-and-breakfast, or dormitory was *built to do something else*: house a family, or students at school. Only incidentally is it a lodging for travelers, and therein lies the difference.

Assuming that you have rights in a desirable location, you can go about the business of making connections. This can be done through classified ads in publications you know and enjoy, which is a good way to contact like-minded people. *The New York Review of Books,* for example, has a column of classifieds for house-swapping which is frequently consulted by academics and literati. The advantage here is not only that like-minded people will be trustworthy (though there's never any guarantee), but also that they will want to go where you live and vice-versa. Look in the back pages of magazines and newspapers you receive to see if there are possibilities for home swaps. Also try through organizations and clubs you've joined. Perhaps a foreign branch will scout leads for you, or post notices.

HOME-EXCHANGE ORGANIZATIONS: If all else fails, apply to a home-swapping organization such as **Vacation Exchange Club, Inc.,** 350 Broadway, New York, NY 10013 (tel. 212/966-2576). The club publishes a directory which lists in detail properties like your own which are available for a swap. *It does not make swap arrangements or guarantee against mishaps*. You pay $21 for the directory, published in two parts in February and April, or $29 if you wish to print a photo of your property. For $14 you can order the directory without including your own notice in it. The VEC has other services in its symbol-filled directory, too. You can find bed-and-breakfast possibilities and some rental properties. Write to the club for full information, and be ready to submit your application before December 15th (press deadline for the February edition) or February 15th (press deadline for the April edition) if you wish your notice to be included.

If you're apprehensive about swapping homes, *Your Place and Mine* by Cindy Gum, available from Gum Publications, 15195 El Camino Grande, Suite 100, Saratoga, CA 95070, will help you organize such exchanges and avoid most of the pitfalls.

TIME-SHARING ORGANIZATIONS: As for time-sharing, you can find out more by writing to the **Resort Timesharing Council**, 1000 16th St. NW, Suite 604, Washington, DC 20036 (tel. 202/659-4582). Include a stamped, self-addressed envelope of business size for a copy of their free fact sheet.

Before you buy your time-sharing property, you should inquire about exchange plans and possibilities. Are you in the very early stages of considering time-sharing? Then write for information to the organizations which operate the most widespread exchange plans: **Interval International**, 7000 S.W. 62nd Ave., Suite 306, Miami, FL 33143 (tel. 305/666-1861 or 800/828-8200); **Resort Condominiums International**, P.O. Box 80229, Indianapolis, IN 46240 (tel. 317/846-4724 or 800/428-6169). By the way, you should know that your annual time-sharing swap may cost you upward of $80 because you must pay a membership fee in the exchange organization, and then pay a fee for their arrangement of the swap. This cost is above and beyond any normal maintenance fees you must pay on your time-sharing property.

"Self-Catering" Accommodations

"Self-catering" is the British term for housekeeping accommodations. Renting a cottage, villa, or kitchen-equipped room is very popular with the British, who have a vast network of rental cottages, brokers, information sources, and customers. The reason is simple. Renting accommodations without service (no bell-hops, chambermaids, desk clerks, janitors, or elevator operators to pay) is good profit for the renter and inexpensive housing for the traveler.

In general, you can save money by directing your efforts to finding accommodations in a building that was *not* built *primarily* to house travelers.

Self-catering accommodations exist throughout the world. The advantages are that you get lots of space to yourself, the chance to save money by cooking your own meals, and as a bonus, your accommodations are frequently charming and offer a unique way of experiencing the country and its people. The disadvantages: rentals tend to be long-term only, at least a week, probably a fortnight (two weeks), preferably a month or more. Also, you are effectively tied down to the immediate surroundings of your rental cottage—you've got to come "home" each night. In England, however, with so much beauty and so many sights of interest within such a small space, this is hardly a disadvantage.

In North America, rental cottages and housekeeping or "efficiency" rooms in hotels, motels, and country inns are also widely available. In years to come, these lodgings will become even more important as hotel prices continue to rise. Sources of information, and clearinghouses for rentals, will expand and amplify, making it easier to rent quickly, at long distance. For now, here are some tips on finding the self-catering accommodation you want, where and when you want it:

Sit down and decide what you want:

Exact arrival and departure dates
Amount you want to pay
General location
Number of rooms
Number of beds
Walking distance to transport, markets, beach

Get source materials. Many magazines and newspapers carry self-catering rental advertisements in their classified ads. The more local the publication and distribution, the more local the ads. But in any internationally distributed magazine or newspaper you can find ads for properties in many parts of the world.

Some guides to self-catering rental properties do exist, but they're difficult to find. An example: Farm Holiday Publications Ltd., 18 High Street, Paisley, Scotland (tel. 041-889-8455), publishes a series of guides on farm holidays (where you stay with a farm family), self-catering rentals, and bed-and-breakfast establishments in England, Scotland, and Wales. Some of their books are sold at the British Travel Bookshop, 680 Fifth Avenue, New York NY 10019.

The British Tourist Authority, 64 St. James's Street, London SW1A 1NF (tel. 01-629-9191), publishes a booklet called *Holiday Homes*, which has listings of many rental apartments in Britain's tourist areas, and costs under $2. Another booklet, *Apartments in London*, is free of charge. It lists not only rental flats in

London, but also the names of agencies which handle rentals—an agency might be able to find what you're looking for if you are unsuccessful. Order these two publications from the British Travel Bookshop, mentioned above, or from British Gifts, Box 26558, Los Angeles, CA 90026; or British Market Inc., 2366 Rice Boulevard, Houston, TX 77005; or Academic Press, 55 Barber Greene Road, Don Mills, ON M3C 2AL. Add $1 for postage and handling.

For other areas and countries, write to the tourist authorities (as outlined in Chapter 3; see Appendix 1 for addresses) and ask them for tips on finding self-catering accommodations.

While the fancy "country inn" a block away is charging $95 a night for hyped-up "charm and atmosphere," the lady who runs the guest house will ask $14 for two, and will offer authentic warmth in the bargain.

Write to the agent or owner for the specifics. Send your list of requirements and a self-addressed envelope, stamped if you're sending it to a place in your own country, or with an IRC (International Reply Coupon, sold at all post offices) if you're sending it abroad. Ask for photos, which you should return to the agent or owner after you've looked at them. Arranging for a flat or villa can take time, especially if you must do it through the international mails—it may take you a month just to write and to receive a reply. Also, the most popular periods will be booked in advance, so get your bid in as early as possible.

Don't let your imagination run away with you. By all means, dream about how much fun you'll have, the walks you'll take, the beaches you'll comb, the country markets and small-town shops you'll get to know. But don't expect your rental home to be exactly what you imagined it to be. It's not supposed to conform to your dream, it's only supposed to be as advertised. Am I being a killjoy? Well, the biggest disappointment renters face is when their quaint Elizabethan thatched cottage in Shakespeare Country turns out to be a tile-roofed guest house in a suburb of Stratford-upon-Avon. The picture showed the front of the house, but not the roof? Then don't imagine a thatched roof. The picture showed the outside, which was quaint and cozy, but not the inside? Perhaps the interior is all spiffy-modern, white walls and streamlined furniture, which happens to be the owner's conception of the Good Life. When selecting a rental place, *be conscious of what you don't know*, to avoid disappointment. What you want is expectations and dreams based on what you do know; the rest is adventure, and unless you actively set yourself up for disappointment, you're sure to enjoy the adventure. Keep an open mind until you can "feel" the place and try it on for size.

The savings? Two people who plan to dine out a lot are not the best candidates for big savings when it comes to self-catering rentals. Families are the big savers. But if a couple nibbles breakfast in the kitchen, prepares most lunches as picnics, and cooks the occasional dinner—or more—at home, they will still save substantially over the cost of equivalent standardized lodgings and meals. You must compare prices on a weekly or monthly basis. If you'd expect to spend $40 or $50 per night on room and breakfast, plus about $20 or $30 daily for lunch and dinner—and these prices are *not high* in many North American tourist areas, nor in Europe—then your weekly costs would be $420 to

$560. You can spend the same amount, but dine more elegantly in more expensive restaurants, by cutting lodging costs with a self-catering rental, or you can spend a smaller total amount by getting a rental and cooking at least some meals for yourself.

VACATION RENTAL ORGANIZATIONS: Self-catering accommodations can be anything from a castle to a travel trailer. In England, for example, two firms will rent you a fixed-base trailer at bargain rates. Contact them for specifications and prices: **Butlin's Travel Service,** 441 Oxford St., London W1A 1BH (tel. 01-499-1313); or **Hoseasons Holidays Ltd.,** Sunway House, 89 Bridge Road, Oulton Broad, Lowestoft, Suffolk NR32 2LT, England (tel. 0502-62270).

Stateside firms which arrange vacation rentals in Europe include **Interchange Vacation Rentals,** 213 East 38th Street, New York, NY 10016 (tel. 212/685-4340; out west, dial 213/271-0575). They list over 20,000 European and Caribbean rentals.

Inquiline, Cedar Rd., Katonah, NY 10536 (tel. 914/232-7516), specializes in rentals in Europe—mainly France, Italy, Spain, Ireland, and Britain with weekly prices ranging from $400 for an Irish cottage to $5000 for a villa in the Dordogne.

Two other organizations are: **Interhome Inc.,** 297 Knollwood Rd., White Plains, NY 10607 (tel. 914/683-9477); **At Home Abroad,** 405 East 56th St., New York, NY 10022 (tel. 212/421-9165).

If you don't want to be bothered with organizations, listings, application forms, etc., many guides are available. For example, *French Farm and Village Holiday Guide* published annually, describes and illustrates 1000 cottages and farmhouses throughout France whose standards are guaranteed by the French government. Copies are available in bookstores or from Unipub, 345 Park Ave. South, New York, NY 10010.

Servas

Servas is an organization that seeks to further international understanding. It sponsors a worldwide program of exchange hospitality for travelers in 80 countries including the U.S. Here's how it works: you apply and are interviewed; if accepted, you get a personal briefing, written instructions, a list of Servas hosts in the area you are going to visit, and an introductory letter. You arrange visits in advance with your host. The usual stay is two nights. For information, write to the U.S. Servas Committee, Inc., 11 John St., Room 406, New York, NY 10038. Servas asks for a donation of $30 for its services.

University Accommodations

The crush of visitors to certain cities at certain times of year produces an abundant crop of nonstandard accommodations. Local officials, attempting to deal with the influx of people, look all over for the essentials: rooms, beds, simple meals. University housing, often empty for weeks or months at a time, is a perfect candidate to be converted to temporary transient housing. The university makes a few dollars on its buildings, and you get a cheap, simple, clean, safe place to stay.

Availability of dorm rooms is very changeable. The only way to be sure that dorm rooms exist in a given city at a given time is to call or write. You may have to reserve in advance, though few places will hold you to this if you look respectable, appear on their doorstep, and they have a room free.

Use the telephone book, or, if you're looking in another state or country go to the library and use their resources. Or better yet, consult the CIEE'S *"Where to Stay USA,"* available in book stores or from CIEE, 205 East 42nd St., New York, NY 10017.

THE REALLY CHEAP OPTIONS

Youth Hostels

You have to be willing to accept sexually segregated dormitory accommodations to stay in a youth hostel, because that's what most of them have: girls' dorms and boys' dorms. You may have to help with the chores of keeping the hostel tidy. You may find that you can't enter the hostel before 5 p.m., and must leave it by 10 a.m. the next morning, even if you're staying several days. And you may find a three-night maximum stay regulation in busy seasons.

Self-catering accommodations exist throughout the world. The advantages are that you get lots of space to yourself, the chance to save money by cooking your own meals, and as a bonus your accommodations are frequently charming and offer a unique way of experiencing the country and its people.

What you get in return is a clean, friendly place to stay at the lowest possible price. Inexpensive but nourishing meals may be available as a bonus; there may be simple cooking facilities so you can prepare your own food. A youth hostel is about the best place in the world to ask questions, scan notice-boards, and pick up the most current information on budget travel.

In some Third World countries, youth hostels are pretty much of a disappointment. Find out the situation first before planning a hosteling trip to such a place.

Membership is currently $7 for under-18s, $14 for adults. For more information, write the American Youth Hostels National Office, 1332 I St., NW, Suite 800, Washington, DC 20005 (tel. 800/424-9426). Also be aware that the Youth Hostels Association offers some very low-cost tours in the United States and abroad (for example, a bicycle tour through China). Programs are outlined in their *Highroad to Adventure* booklet, available from the address above.

YMCA's and YWCA's

Part of the purpose of the Ys is to provide basic, decent accommodations: you can't host a business meeting or hold a convention at a Y. A few are unsuitable, but in general the Ys provide decent if spartan rooms (mostly singles) for a very low price, throughout much of the world.

In Hartford, the YWCA is a modern highrise, much like a good hotel with its cafeteria, rooms-with-bath which have a fine view of the state capitol, and sports facilities. In Jerusalem the YMCA is a mammoth pseudo-Oriental palace with many rooms, indoor pool, cafeteria, game and sports rooms, even lectures and entertainment. In Montreal, the YMCA and YWCA both have superb downtown locations plus comfortable, though unglamorous, facilities.

A "Y" room may have a television set, or even a private bathroom. Often you have a choice, and you needn't pay for these if you don't want them. In general, YMCA's accept both men and women as guests, while YWCA's accept women only. The main problem with Ys is that the rooms offer such value for money that they are often booked solid by residents. If you write ahead though, you can usually get a room.

Want more information? Contact the YMCA, 356 West 34th Street, New York, NY 10001 (tel. 212/760-5856); same address for the YWCA.

Camping

Anyplace to which large numbers of people can drive will have camping facilities. This means that you can contemplate a camping tour anywhere in Europe and North America, but not in Central Africa, or the Caribbean.

There is an exception to this general rule though—you can pitch a tent, and stay a while, on St. John, U.S. Virgin Islands, at Cinnamon Bay National Park (P.O. Box 120, Cruz Bay; tel. 776-6330) and on Tortola, British Virgin Islands, at Brewer's Bay (P.O. Box 185, Road Town; tel. 4-3463).

University housing, often empty for weeks or months at a time, is a perfect candidate to be converted to temporary transient housing. The university makes a few dollars on its buildings, and you get a cheap, simple, clean, safe place to stay.

The U.S. National Park Service system offers unique and spectacular settings for camping trips. You can get an overview of the possibilities throughout the U.S. by sending for the *Guide and Map for National Parks* to the U.S. Department of the Interior, National Park Service, Washington, DC 20240. You can even reserve ahead in at least seven national parks through any Ticketron agency.

For private campgrounds *Woodall's* is a comprehensive directory with listings of campgrounds in the U.S. and Canada; experienced campers swear by it.

You must think of camping as more than roughing it with a nylon tent and a backpack. Modern tents which pop open in a few minutes, sleeping bags and pads of space-age materials, highly organized camping areas equipped with showers, laundromats, shops, sports grounds, even restaurants and entertainment—all these make camping much easier and more comfortable than your traditional idea of life in the wilderness.

The very easiest camping of all is in a well-equipped van. No tent to set up, no weather to worry about. Often one can just pull off the road or park near a beach, and the cost of an overnight stay is nearly nothing.

In many countries you can rent camper vans, large campers, or trailers. They are not cheap, though, and you should add up all costs very carefully before arranging a rental. Oftentimes, buying a used camper is a much better idea, as used campers retain a high proportion of their value from year to year. As with a car, if you sell the van in the same year you buy it, and if you haven't run it into the ground, you may recover the purchase price completely.

Once-in-a-while camping is a possibility for serendipitous travelers who may find their funds running low or are in a place where accommodations are hard to find. If you've had the foresight to stow a small tent and air mattresses in the car (along with your picnic supplies), you can have that fail-safe option for a night or two.

In some countries, camping has become as convenient as staying in a motel. Israel, for example, has a system of established campsites where you rent a tent (already pitched) and cots just as you would a motel room.

Taking it one stage further, there are now companies offering camping tours, most often through Europe. The price of the tour usually includes meals, transportation, and equipment. It makes an ideal trip for the young at heart or solo traveler who is visiting Europe for the first time. Check with your travel agent, and keep camping in mind while gathering information on your destination.

11

Savvy Dining

What you pay for sustenance is one of the Big Three travel expenses, along with transportation and lodging. When you purchase food, you want to get the best value for your money in terms of both nutrition and enjoyment. You can fine-tune your eating habits to get the most for your money. Here's how:

THE FOUR BASIC LAWS

Follow the four basic laws of the budget traveler when it comes to food:

1. Eat well to stay healthy. Sickness and distress are not only unpleasant, they are expensive. They rob you of vacation time and vacation money.
2. Dine according to the customs of the country. If you do this, you will eat better, and more, and you will spend the same—or less—than a local person does for food.
3. Lunch is cheaper than dinner.
4. Plan ahead to prepare at least half of your meals yourself.

153

Eat Well to Stay Healthy

Some people think this simply means not starving yourself. Not only must you eat enough, many times you will find you must eat more because of your increased level of activity. Get enough food. Also, have regular meals. And choose those foods which will give you the greatest nutritional value for the money. Don't order a soft drink with your sandwich, order milk. Milk is virtually a complete food, whereas soda is a mixture of water, sugar, flavor, and caffeine. Often a glass of milk costs *less* than a glass of soda.

KNOW YOUR NUTRITION: If you know nothing about nutrition, learn something before you go away, so that you can make intelligent decisions. One can easily drop into a hamburger stand and spend $5 or $6 on foods of questionable value: "milkshakes" which contain little milk, but lots of sugar, salt, and chemicals; fried side orders (french fries, fried onion rings) which pound-for-pound are more expensive than filet mignon; sodas, cookies, and sweet desserts. But a hamburger stand is not necessarily a "junk food" dispensary, though it is a "fast food" one. Look at what's in the normal chain-restaurant hamburger: bread, beef, tomato, lettuce, pickled cucumber. Add a slice of cheese, some mayonnaise (one needs edible oils), and relish, and you have a decently balanced light meal. It is not "health food," but it is basically quite nutritious. And the cost for this balanced mini-meal? About $2. Have a hamburger or cheeseburger and milk. Look upon the french fries and milkshakes as rather perilous forms of entertainment, but not as valuable foods.

Your knowledge of nutrition will come in handier abroad, where the standard hamburger may not be available. Faced with a Turkish breakfast table, what would you see? Hard-boiled eggs (perhaps nature's most perfect food), black olives, salty white cheese (the salt helps retain your fluids in the hot, dry summer), bread and jam, *su boreği* (a flaky pastry filled with cheese and herbs), fruit juices, and a cauldron of *sicak süt.* (warm milk with sugar). Protein, carbohydrates, edible oils, vitamins—they're all here, just take your pick. You won't find bacon in a Moslem country. Bacon, like french fries, is an entertainment, not a food. This brings us to the second law:

Copy Local Dining Habits

Dine according to the customs of the country. This means that you must not only eat *what* the locals eat, but eat it *when* and *where* they eat it. A good example: orange juice at breakfast. Countries without the bounty of Florida and California have not developed the custom of having orange juice at breakfast all year long. If you order it specially, it will cost like the dickens. You may pass a fresh juice stand on the street, and it may be citrus season—in that case orange juice makes sense. Or keep an eye out for neighborhood greengrocers—where you can buy oranges or other high-Vitamin C fruits for a pick-me-up snack. If the local people show no signs of scurvy, they're getting their Vitamin C daily, and you can too, at the same affordable prices they're paying.

Butter is another example. Few countries look upon butter as a necessary table condiment. Having butter on the table morning, noon, and night would seem to them like our having a bowl of whipped cream always in sight. You can get butter anywhere. You will pay dearly for it.

You'll be surprised at how much you can save not only by eating what local people do, but also *where* they eat. In most countries of southern Europe (Italy, France, Spain), for example, you'll notice that restaurants do not include coffee on their special three-course tourist menu (it's rarely on the menu at all). It is customary there to drink coffee at a separate bar/café rather than in a restaurant that serves food. And that means not only after-dinner but also breakfast coffee. So head for a bar/café for delicious morning-fresh rolls and breakfast coffee to start your day in a most enjoyable, very European manner.

Dine according to the customs of the country. This means that you must not only eat *what* the locals eat, but also eat it *when* and *where* they eat it.

You'll save considerably. Even here in the United States, working people will drop into a deli for coffee and a roll, croissant, bagel, etc.; such a breakfast may cost you $1.25; a comparable one will cost you at least twice as much at your hotel. Similarly, in Britain, the working folk go to the pubs for lunch and it's here that you'll find the best food values and most authentic local snacks and dishes as well as the jovial company of the "locals." As a general rule, avoid hotel dining, especially for lunch and breakfast. A hotel coffeeshop will often charge double the price of a similar establishment two blocks from the hotel.

FOLLOW THE RHYTHM: Also, get used to the *rhythm* of eating in a foreign country. In England, big breakfast, light pub lunch, light snacks at teatime, late moderate supper. In Mexico, light breakfast, large late lunch, light supper. To find out the customs of the country, ask about them. Everyone likes to talk about food, dining, local delicacies, and habits. They'll give you rapturous discourses on dishes their mothers used to make, on a favorite local chef's specialties, on the richness of the country's produce.

**COMMUNICATE YOUR WILLINGNESS TO EXPERI-
MENT:** Local people will assume you want your own
sort of food. You must get around this. In Cairo's
better hotels one finds almost exclusively Western
food (at Western prices). The Western food is prepared by Eastern chefs who don't care for it and never
eat it. This Western food is at best mediocre, at worst
godawful. In a local Cairo restaurant you can stuff
yourself on shish kebab, *kafta, ful,* and *taamiya*
(skewered lamb, grilled spiced ground meat, savory
beans, and bean fritters) for the price of a single bottle
of beer at the Hilton.

In asking about food, approach someone this way:
instead of "I'm thirsty, I need a Coke," say, "I'm
thirsty—what do local people drink?" You may end up
with refreshing tea with mint, or fruit juice, or spring
water.

Lunch Is Cheaper Than Dinner

Why is lunch cheaper than dinner, virtually everywhere in the world? It's simple: millions of people eat
lunch away from home, but many fewer eat dinner
away from home. Dinner is a discretionary meal: you
can dine at home *or* in a restaurant. At lunchtime,
however, most people are going about their day's work
and would rather not traipse all the way home to eat.
Local restaurants can depend on great volume, and
can therefore offer more for less. The Business Lunch
is now a world institution: a set-price, multi-course
repast designed to attract office workers with good and
plenteous food at moderate prices. If you only buy one
meal a day, it probably should be lunch.

LOW-COST LUNCHES: Workers eat cheaply, and
whether you're in Stockholm, London, Paris, or
Rome, you'll find appetizing lunches at the least expensive prices at these insiders' restaurants. In England, of course, pubs traditionally offer simple, hearty

fare. For French regional cooking at its finest, stop in at a *routier,* roughly comparable to the U.S. truck stop or roadside diner, distinguished by the traditional routier's white disk-like sign in front. In Rome, labor unions and branches of the military have centrally located restaurants, and Stockholm has its "bars," which are popular cafeteria-like establishments (there's one in the central city park).

Department stores provide a good source for inexpensive lunches or snacks. And at Paris's Samaritaine store, the view from the terrace cafe supplies a city backdrop that outdoes any of that city's four-star restaurants.

Do-It-Yourself Dining

Plan ahead to prepare at least half of your meals yourself. "Oh," you say to yourself, "how sordid! Here I am in my room, eating cheese, bread, sausage off a plastic bag!" It's your own fault if your impromptu meal is no gourmet's delight. The ingredients for an elegant picnic are probably just around the corner in the local market, but you didn't plan ahead or think creatively. You just bought a lump of some strange cheese, and an entire loaf of bread (of which you will throw three-fourths away), and too much of a sausage you don't really care for.

EVERYBODY DOES IT: At the very moment you are lamenting your plight, travelers all over the world are sitting down to picnics in their rooms. *Every* traveler eats in his room. *No one* likes eating in restaurants and snack shops all the time. The truth is that it's relaxing to be out of the struggle with waiters, strange dishes, worry about prices, mistakes on bills, concern over tipping, finding a good place. Your mistake is not that you're eating in your room; your mistake is that you did not plan the meal properly.

A traveler is certainly limited when it comes to buying foodstuffs. Large items (whole melons, cuts of meat, pounds of pasta), items which must be prepared with utensils (ovens, colanders, frying pans, toasters, grinders), items which need constant refrigeration, or which can't take travel easily (fish, fresh eggs, many fruits and vegetables) are all out of the question for the traveler's picnic. But even a modest meal need not be boring if you prepare for it.

A DO-IT-YOURSELF PICNIC: Take a bag for shopping: set aside some time specifically for grocery shopping, just as you would before preparing a meal at home. Check through the markets, and shop as though you lived there: ask for a taste of the cheese or the olives, find out what's in the sausages, watch the locals buying bread. Does the bakery sell rolls? Does it sell half- and quarter-loaves? (In most countries with fresh-baked bread, bakeries sell a variety of sizes of loaves, or they will gladly sell you only a portion—they do it all the time.) Alternatives to bread include dry rusks (zwieback), plain crackers, unleavened bread.

Lunch is cheaper than dinner. . . . If you
only buy one meal a day, it probably
should be lunch.

Note: Besides purchasing your picnic fare at the markets you can often find delectable stand-up meals in or on the fringes of the market—spicy hot leberkase and all kinds of wurst in Germany, hot tempting pizza in Italy, stir-fried vegetables and noodles from a cook-boat in Bangkok, or crisp fried pork cracklings with salsa verde at the massive market in Mexico City.

Back in your room, set up your meal just as you would at home. Have utensils (plastic ones from the plane will do; metal is nicer, but heavier), napkins, glasses (from the bathroom shelf), a bottle of wine, fresh wildflowers or a candle. Dining is a ceremony, and the best dinners are made not with just good cooking, but with pleasant ritual as well. You may then feast on simple fare: good cheese, an interesting cold meat, pickled olives or vegetables, preserved seafood (sardines, pickled fish, canned oysters or octopus), nutritious raw vegetables and fruits, a glass or two of mineral water or the local table wine.

In places where good foodstuffs are abundant, you can truly feast. A Paris market yielded the following cheap hotel room feast for my wife and me: *crudités* (raw vegetables with a dash of salt and vinegar), *terrine de lapin* (a delicious rabbit pâté), *pâté de faisan* (pheasant pâté), fresh camembert and *fromage de chèvre* (creamy, flavorful goatsmilk cheese), *clemantine* (seedless tangerines), and *dattes de Tunisie farci* (dried Tunisian dates stuffed with walnuts). We accompanied our feast first with a cup of hot bouillon, then with an inexpensive local wine, and finished up with French coffee and cognac. How much would such a meal have cost in a Parisian restaurant? About $20 apiece. How much did we pay? About $5 each.

Think "picnic" when you're sightseeing, too. Even in the heart of great cities there are parks, both large and "vest-pocket," where you can have a picnic lunch. Outside the cities, châteaux, castles, and other tourist attractions provide very pleasant picnic sites for their visitors. But even if there are no specific picnic areas on your route, you'll soon become adept at spotting likely picnic spots—along a grassy river bank, at scenic mountain overlooks—even the ramparts of a medieval city can serve as your dining table.

BE PREPARED FOR YOUR PICNICS: You may want to build a small supply of kitchen tools, taking some from home and picking up others along the way. A multipurpose pocket knife with a corkscrew, such as a Swiss army knife, is good to have, plus a can opener; vegetable peeler, paper napkins, eating utensils, stores of a few spices and such condiments as salt, pepper, sugar, bouillon cubes, etc. A fine piece of screening or cloth, or an infusion ball ("tea egg") will allow you to make tea and coffee without leaves or grounds left in the cup. If you can stand instant, use that.

A tool we find indispensable is an immersion heater coil. Pick one up in a North American hardware or grocery store ($2 or $3) for 110 voltage and domestic trips. For the rest of the world, look for one abroad that operates on 220 volts, and keep it for later trips. I was appalled some years ago when I found a good sturdy 220-volt immersion heater in Greece—it cost an astounding $8! But since I bought it, that coil has heated water for about 1,000,000 cups of coffee, tea, bouillon, chicken noodle soup, hot toddies, sleeping potions (hot milk with honey), sore throat remedies (hot tea with lemon and honey), shaving when there's only a cold water tap, even mulled wine (cheap red wine, orange slices, raisins, cinnamon stick).

SOME FINAL PICNIC TIPS: As you explore your travel destination, pick up bits of information which will help you to prepare your meals: detour into shops for ideas of what's available, ask locals to point out the nearest bakery, wine shop, grocery store, or market. Are there open-air markets? What are the market days? What local foods are good for a picnic? Is there a delicatessen, *charcuterie,* etc., in the neighborhood? Bring your supplies home inconspicuously so the hotel clerk doesn't raise a fuss. Clean up, and the clerk will never know.

Remember: everybody is eating in their rooms; a good meal must be prepared, not thrown together; make it a ceremony, however informal; relax, and enjoy the luxury of dining with your shoes off, at your own pace, without having to flag down waiters or tot up restaurant bills—and at a fraction of the price.

GETTING THE MOST OUT OF A RESTAURANT

No one eats in restaurants all the time, but no one eats at home all the time either. For those occasions when you want to or must buy a meal, you should know that there are ways to get the maximum for your money.

Choosing a Restaurant

Finding the right restaurant is the most important step of all. Guidebooks, advertisements, a hotel concierge or clerk will all give you advice, but you won't know the restaurant is truly worthwhile until after you've eaten there. By then, it may be too late.

The greatest problem comes with standards. "Where's a good, cheap place to eat?" Well now, what does "good" mean to you? Definitions of good range from "I don't care so long as I don't gag and the portions are huge" to "The waiter must be all in black, of course, and the *quenelles* must come on a warm— but not hot—plate." Both definitions are valid. Just beware when you are using one and your advisor is using the other.

Of course your advisor is going to recommend a "good" restaurant. No one wants to rush off to a "bad" or "mediocre" restaurant, so avoid the word "good" completely when asking for a place to dine. Instead, be specific: how close is it, what does it serve, is there atmosphere, how much does an average meal cost? Have you eaten there, how long ago? Who eats there, tourists or locals? What are the other choices?

GET SEVERAL RECOMMENDATIONS: Get not one but several recommendations, and soon you will see a pattern emerge: no one has ever come away from the Grumbling Gravy dissatisfied; the Caviar-and-Cress is only for the expense account crowd; the Fish Vat's food is not refined, but portions are big and prices are low. One meal in one restaurant is very scant evidence upon which to base a universal judgment. By asking many people, you get the benefit of judgments by different judges who have dined there on different nights at varying times in the past.

Few countries look upon butter as a necessary table condiment. Having butter on the table morning, noon, and night would seem to them like our having a bowl of whipped cream always in sight. You can get butter anywhere. You will pay dearly for it.

Watch for self-interest: the desk clerk who gets a kickback, or who comes up with the same name for every guest; or the obliging soul who sends you where he thinks you want to go—to the place where all foreigners go (perhaps McDonald's or Kentucky Fried Chicken), rather than where he would go himself.

Checking It Out

Now that you've got some leads, go check the place out. Is there a menu posted outside the door? If not, no matter. March in and ask to see one. Don't sit down, just stand out of the way and read it near the door. No one will mind, and if they do it's a sure sign that the place is lousy. (I've had waiters at the Ritz bring a menu to the door so I could read it, which they did very graciously.)

Next: is it busy? Should it be? If it's empty in a busy downtown area at lunchtime, or in a resort on Saturday evening, those vacant places are shouting a warning at you. You can try it, but don't expect much.

Don't *ever* be afraid to get up and walk out if your sensors tell you that you're in for something that you won't enjoy. If you have ordered something, you should feel obligated to pay for it. But if you haven't ordered, you are free to leave, no matter how many glasses of water have been poured or napkins unfolded. Waiters are used to people leaving, especially in clip joints and bad places; even in good places it happens, as potential diners discover they "really wanted something fancier/cheaper, serving seafood/vegetarian food, with/without a liquor license."

Another assertion of your rights: get a good table. Be understanding of the waiter's responsibilities, and don't monopolize a prime four-seat window table if you're alone; but also don't accept a table by the kitchen door or the silverware racks or the cash register, or in a draft, or right beneath the Muzak, if there is an acceptable alternative. What you pay for your meal will be exactly the same whether you dine in the wind from the swinging door, or at that cozy spot by the crackling fire. Get your money's worth.

Restaurant Bargain Days

In much of the world, including North America, there is a specific weekly rhythm to restaurant life, dictated by the society's general lifestyle. Friday and Saturday are the busiest nights, Sunday afternoon is not bad. Monday is the traditional closing day, though many restaurants will serve lunch for the business clientele. In fact, lunch Monday through Friday is fairly well attended; many places won't even serve lunch on Saturday or Sunday, only dinner.

What happens Tuesday and Wednesday evenings? Not much. Everybody in town is deep into the work week, and few people have the time or inclination for a big dinner with drinks and wine—they've got to get up early and be in top shape for a Wednesday- or Thursday-morning conference.

Tuesday and Wednesday evenings are thus the best times to look for bargain dinners. Astute restaurateurs will offer good if simple values on these evenings to attract more customers. Often the value will be an extra-lavish set-price meal, or a normal meal at a discounted price.

You may even find a chance to haggle: standing at the door perusing the menu, a waiter (with time on his hands) may wander over and engage you in conversation, hoping to bring you in and seat you.

"Lots of good things on that menu," he says.

"Sure," you say, "but prices are a little high for our budget; we'd have to forego having wine with dinner."

"Hold on a minute," he says, and disappears. When he emerges, it is to say, "The chef will provide a carafe of house wine, on the house." Point of Mutual Advantage: the restaurant keeps its staff busy and *fills a table* (full tables lure other customers) in exchange for a few dollars' markup on the wine, while you get the meal you wanted, with free wine. All you did was make it easy for them to be generous. Everybody's happy.

How to Identify the Best Values on a Menu

Are all menus created equal? Of course not. What are the differences? How is a menu made?

A restaurateur wants a list of dishes which will both appeal to a large clientele and yield him a profit. The price charged for a particular dish may or may not reflect the cost of its preparation; it may or may not reflect the dish's quality and nutritional value.

Which offers the best value-for-money? A huge chef's salad for $5, or a plate of spaghetti for the same? Which costs more to make? On which is the profit the biggest?

Where is quality going to be the highest? In Texas cattle country, on steaks or seafood? The beef probably walked to the back door. The lobster was caught weeks ago in Maine, frozen like a rock, and brought by Boeing to the Texas restaurant's freezer.

THE BASIC STRATEGY: Here is my strategy for ordering from a menu, developed by long experience of restaurant-sampling. First, compare the menu with foods available in the region, giving preference to native ones. Try to remember which foods are in season, such as vegetables, fruits, game, shellfish, and fish. Ordering foods which are out of season means you will get lower quality, or higher prices, or both. If you've been following my advice and preparing some of your own meals, you know what's fresh in the markets.

Next, try to figure out which dishes are there to make a profit and which are there to make life interesting for the chef. Surf-and-Turf, the popular small steak and lobster tail, is simple to prepare from frozen ingredients, and always carries a high price tag. Several other items at the top of the price range will be there for the same reason: not because they are particularly fine, but because they are exotic, or out of season, or chic, or because unselective diners are captive to them, as in "I want a big, juicy steak." Except in good steak houses, steak is usually on the menu to make a profit from people who will eat nothing but steak.

THE DAILY SPECIAL—YOUR BEST BET: The chef gets no creative thrill from preparing surf-and-turf, or steak. He or she gets her kicks from delicate and interesting preparations, and from the items on the menu which change: the daily specials.

In the average, low- to middle-range restaurant, the menu might as well be carved in granite, except for the daily specials. The standard list of items is easy to store and prepare (freezer, microwave, etc.) and makes a good profit. The daily specials, or *prix fixe* meal, or *comida corrida,* or whatever it's called, is where the chef has fun and adds variety to her life. She buys less of the ingredients than she knows she can sell (tomorrow's special will be different—she wants today's to sell out and not take up storage room), so you're guaranteed freshness. She takes interest in its preparation. And she puts a price on the special which will guarantee not only a decent return, but also that it will sell out. By far, the daily special meal offers the best value for money. If you choose from the standard menu, you pay for the privilege whether the food is excellent or indifferent.

In a local Cairo restaurant you can stuff yourself on shish kebab, *kafta, ful,* and *taamiya* (skewered lamb, grilled spiced meat, savory beans, and bean fritters) for the price of a single bottle of beer at the Hilton.

Another selling point: daily specials are the dishes made from highly perishable ingredients such as fresh shrimp, or unusual ingredients which come into the market that day but are gone the next.

If there are no daily specials, the chef is dead or is not a chef. Or, locals never go to that restaurant. Locals demand variety.

Beware the six-page, handsomely printed, lavishly illustrated menu. If it offers an astounding array of dishes, it's likely that none of them will be fresh or tasty. In my experience the meals I've liked best were in restaurants where there were about six dinner-entree specials, with an even fewer number of appetizers and desserts. Each of the offerings was freshly prepared with loving attention, and was well worth its price. No restaurant can adequately handle many different kinds of dishes without suffering an accompanying loss of quality. In assessing a restaurant's menu, remember, less is more.

HOW MUCH WILL IT COST?

Want to estimate the total price of the meal before you sit down? Choose a main course you like, and double the price of it. If you want drinks before dinner or a bottle (not a carafe) of wine with your meal, add a bit more. Here's an illustration:

Notice that the tip is about 11%. To believe that 15% is required is silly. To give 20% is outrageous unless service has been spectacular. To give less than 10% borders on insult (which may be what you want to do). Average, as far as I'm concerned, is 10% to 12%, with 15% the reward for quite good service. In many foreign countries, percentages are much lower except in tourist joints.

	cumulative cost
Soup or appetizer, $1.50 to $2.50	about $ 2
Main course: filet of sole, $10	12
Cheese or dessert, $2	14
Coffee, $1	15
Large glass of wine, $2	17
Meal tax, $1	18
Tip, $2	$20

One further point about tipping: always check on the menu before you order to see whether or not the service is included in the total price. That way you won't be embarrassed by having to ask the waiter after you've received the check or by having to ask to see the menu again.

Adding Up the Bill

Always do it. Banks take extreme care in adding up sums of money, and they still make mistakes. A busy restaurant waiter is even less dependable when it comes to figures. Beyond normal human fallibility, there is human cupidity, so your chances of encountering faulty addition, mistaken prices, unwarranted taxes and mysterious extra charges on restaurant bills are actually quite enormous. If you are in doubt, have it explained. If you are still uncertain, appeal to the cashier, maître d', or manager. Are you pretty sure you've been ripped off? Hang around and make a quiet fuss. If the rip-off is real, *they do not want you there*. They want to rip you off quietly and anonymously, and if you are not quiet and anonymous they will give in just to get rid of you. And you win. One thing is certain: you can't travel inexpensively by allowing people to take your money for nothing.

12

Saving Money on Sights and Entertainment

Most travelers spend a modest amount of their travel budget on sightseeing: admission fees to zoos, museums, historic buildings, plus perhaps the occasional sightseeing tour with a guide in a bus. With a lazy approach and timid attitude, one can actually spend a sizable sum on sightseeing. To spend virtually nothing, you need luck as well as foresight and skill. But it is a simple fact that one can visit any major attraction and see the most exciting things for a very modest sum, and for this you don't even need luck.

SIGHTSEEING AT A DISCOUNT

Seeing sights consists of two things: getting there, and getting in. What one pays for each may range from $0 to infinity, which is surprising since sightseeing prices are mostly fixed like iron. How then, can one spend $0 to infinity?

Passes and Packages

Another popular discounting procedure is the all-inclusive pass or package, or "combination ticket." American or Canadian national parks, Newport's grand mansions, England's National Trust properties—these and similar networks offer cut-rate passes which will save you a bundle if you visit more than just one or two.

Some of these sightseeing discounts are available for just one travel season, others have been offered for several years. A long-standing offer from the Netherlands Tourist Office, for example, is the Holland Culture Card, available for $5 to North American residents only. The card permits free entry to over 150 Dutch art and historic museums and other important sites. Also, cardholders can buy reserved seats for concert, ballet, and opera performances up to 24 hours before curtain time. In nearby Belgium, there is a "Brussels Is Love" coupon booklet, with sightseeing discounts for those staying at participating hotels. Another good long-running offer is BritRail Travel's "Open to View" ($19 for adults, $9.50 for children 5 to 15) ticket. This one ticket entitles you to visit an impressive number of Great Britain's most exciting attractions—from the Tower of London to Edinburgh Castle—for a period of one month, starting from the date the ticket is first used.

Local tourism authorities are also zealous in putting together packages and combinations for a particular city or region. In New York City, for example, the Visitors' Bureau publishes a free directory of tour and hotel packages. Their "Ultimate Winter Vacation" package ($198 per person, double occupancy) includes four nights' accommodation, theater tickets, bus or helicopter tour, two dinners, a visit to the Empire State Building, and free maps and other information.

Why do tourism officials dream up these discount schemes to tempt you into their lands? What's in it for them? Mutual advantage, for you will come if they put money in your pocket (which is what they're doing), and you will stay in their hotels and dine in their restaurants and perhaps buy their goods as souvenirs. They are giving you something of value which costs them little: the museums must be kept up no matter how many people visit, and the trains will run whether you are on board or not. Everybody wins.

Family Plans

Tourist authorities recognize that the burden of sightseeing costs is heaviest on families, as two adult and several children's tickets can add up to a hefty sum, particularly if the sight is a theme park (Disney World) or an elaborate "outdoor museum" such as Mystic Seaport or Old Sturbridge Village. Therefore, you will usually find a "family" ticket or a "maximum fee" which will allow you in at a discount. If such a plan doesn't exist, make up your own and try it out on the ticket collector. What do you have to lose? Pay for parents and three kids, and let the other two sneak under the turnstile; or get all the children, even the teenagers, in for the under-10 rate.

Special Discounts

Senior citizens with proof-of-age identification and students with ISIC cards or other student ID can cut sightseeing fees by significant sums. See Chapter 15 for details on how to get these savings. Any traveler going abroad will do well to ask at tourist offices for what nonresident sightseeing discounts are currently available at their destination—in many cases these special discounts are sold only outside the offering country.

FREE ACTIVITIES

Unlike hotels and restaurants, most attractions are not set up to make a profit, and fees will be modest, to cover expenses. In addition, many sights are free. In London, for example, three of the most inspiring and awesome sights—the British Museum, a session of the House of Commons in the Palace of Westminster, and trials at the Old Bailey—are free.

Your duty, then, is to pay no more than the sensible prices for seeing world-famous attractions. There are lots of ways you can pay a bit less, too.

Civic-minded groups sponsor walking tours, architectural tours, historical exhibitions. Municipal authorities will set up outdoor concerts and festivities. Check listings in local newspapers for specific details. Industrial tours can be fun, interesting, even intoxicating (as in the case of the popular brewery tours).

These activities are slightly out of the ordinary, and thus the people you meet at them will be the more interesting and adventurous types. You will almost certainly get to meet local people as well, and you will truly participate in the daily life of the society—a thrilling experience.

Some of the most interesting—and memorable—free travel experiences take a bit of advance planning. Here's how some creative advance planning paid off for two foresighted travelers. A professor of communications at a New York college wrote to the British Broadcasting Corporation before he went to London. When he was in England, he and his wife were given an insider's tour of the broadcast studios. Another creative traveler enjoyed an architectural tour of Seattle with a guide from the area's landmarks commission after she had written to express her interest in exchanging ideas about her favorite topic—historic preservation. Whatever your occupation, field of interest, or hobby, you can locate a counterpart in the place you're going to visit. A brief letter in advance of your trip can be the "open sesame" to the kind of experience no paid tour could possibly offer.

Make Up Your Own Free Adventures

If this paragraph results in your having just one fascinating and unforgettable experience, it will have accomplished its purpose: to get you to overcome language barriers, natural trepidation, and social conventions, and to go on an adventure.

Whatever your occupation, field of interest, or hobby, you can locate a counterpart in the place you're going to visit. A brief letter in advance can be the "open sesame" to the kind of experience no paid tour could possibly offer.

In the beautiful colonial Mexican city of San Luis Potosí, I once passed an ornate and elegant building on a side street. No sign, no clue to its use or purpose was evident. In fact, it was none of my business! But somehow I brought myself to try the door, which was open; somehow I got up the courage to tiptoe in. What I found was an elegant, opulent urban palace, perfectly preserved from a century ago. It was an exclusive men's club, I found out from a servant who approached me—to toss me out, I was sure. Instead of the bums' rush, I got a guided tour! My Spanish was not so good, but I came to understand which was the dining room and which the card room, what local luminaries had belonged here and which exciting events had been played out within the gilded walls. I will never forget it. A minor club in the eyes of the world, but a true Mexican adventure for me. I offered the servant a tip, which he strenuously refused (he had never given a tourist a tour before!).

Do not go where you are not wanted. Don't be impolite. But also don't anticipate hostility when there is none in sight. Oddly enough, it's true that "the best adventures in travel are free."

NIGHTLIFE ON A BUDGET

Nightime activities are among the most fertile areas for cutting costs. For one thing, clubs and shows are in the business to make big profits, and if you're not careful they'll do just that off *you*.

There is hardly a major city in the world today where one cannot have a fascinating night on the town and spend next to nothing. No-cost or low-cost activities are all around you and, when you're in a strange place, they can provide almost as much novelty and excitement as a budget-busting show at the Folies Bergère.

Saving Money on Tickets

Like so many other services today, the market for concert, theater, and show tickets is broken down into segments to yield the greatest return. The most expensive tickets are the ones for the best seats, sold well before the performance, at a ticket agency rather than at the box office. Conversely, the least expensive seats are the ones sold only minutes before the show, at the box office, for whatever seats are left.

Most theaters can predict how many people will just show up on their doorsteps a half hour before the performance; also, they know how many seats have been sold in advance. To assure the least number of empty seats, they begin discounting a certain number of seats the day of the performance. Sometimes the discount sales begin in the morning, sometimes at noon, sometimes a few hours before curtain time. As an out-of-town visitor, these "rush" seats are perfect for you. More often than not, rush seats are sold in a special booth rather than at regular ticket agencies; or they may be sold only from the theater box office itself.

Ask around to find out where rush tickets are sold, and don't rest on the word of just one person. Not everyone knows about them, and many people have an interest in your buying a full-priced seat.

VERY LAST-MINUTE TICKET BARGAINS: Another way to cut the cost of theater and concert tickets is to show up at the hall, circulate through the crowd, and find someone with tickets to sell. The vagaries of illness, broken dates, accidents, and so forth often yield rich pickings for the last-minute ticket buyer. Naturally, the unfortunate ticketholder who wants to recoup his costs will ask for the full price. For a crowded, popular show he might just get it, and so perhaps you'd better grab them. But for a normal performance, get to the hall 30 or 45 minutes before curtain time, identify the people with tickets to sell, and let them know you're in the market. Don't buy, but stand and watch them instead. Are they selling their tickets? Time is on your side, and the price will drop constantly. Right before curtain time, if there are tickets left, you will get any price you mention. Still nothing satisfactory? Curtain time itself, and shortly thereafter, is when the most frantic bargaining takes place. A person running up to the door with unused and (for them) unusable tickets a few minutes after curtain time may even be satisfied with the good feeling of generosity, and give them to you for free.

Clubs and shows are in the business to make big profits, and if you're not careful they'll do just that off *you*.

Don't forget the box office. Depending on policy (and the true policy may only come clear right at curtain time) you may be able to buy cut-price tickets at curtain time or just after. The ticket seller will probably wait until the crowd vacates the lobby. The theater doesn't want it generally known that it sells cheap tickets, when all those other people have paid full price! An important note: no matter how frantic the atmosphere, make sure the money is right. *Count your change carefully* (even slowly, if necessary); if you're doing all this in foreign currency it can be all the more confusing. But don't let anyone rush you. The theater people go through the same routines every night. If they want to rip you off, they'll be experts on how to railroad you through.

Saving Money at the Movies

Cinemas in many countries charge different prices for different times of the day or days of the week. Again, Tuesday and Wednesday are the slow nights. In countries with "early closing," the early closing day (usually Wednesday) features special cinema prices. Everyone gets off from work, and children get out of school, at noon or 1 p.m., and the cinemas would like to attract the business.

Another way to save money on cinema tickets is to look for "People's Day," a special time of the week when tickets sell at reduced prices just as they do at museums. And just like the museums, this cut-price period is often one in which the moviehouse would otherwise be very empty.

In countries with differing prices for the various sections of the theater—"orchestra," "parquet," "balcony," etc.—you needn't buy the most expensive seat for the best view of the screen. Many times the price is high for another reason. The balcony is a favorite spot for romantic encounters and explorations, and local adolescents will pay more for the privilege and privacy. They'll make their own entertainment. Who cares what's on the screen?

Saving Money at Nightclubs

This is tough, because clubs expect you to pay freely. Of course, you should sit or stand at the bar rather than at a table unless you plan to dine. At the World Trade Center in New York, this will save you a $2.75 cover. Often there is no cover charge at the bar, or the charge is smaller, or the minimum is less. If you're single, this is where you'll meet new people in any case.

Clubs are usually quite responsive to supply and demand, eliminating the cover charge on slow nights, or sponsoring a two-drinks-for-the-price-of-one Happy Hour to lure customers. There are occasional opportunities for reductions, if you remember to ask. On busy nights, though, you may actually have trouble getting into a popular club. The bouncer at the door may demand a club membership card or ID. If you don't have one of these, a $5 or $10 bill will do just as well.

13

Shopping for Bargains

The quaint custom of haggling is usually associated with colorful peasants in outdoor markets, bearded patriarchs in Middle Eastern bazaars, or lively Oriental dealers in crowded stall-sized shops. But haggling—like that other "quaint" Third World custom of petty bribery—is something we do frequently here at home. The difference is merely of size and frequency.

No one in his right mind would waltz into an automobile dealership and agree to pay the very first price put to him by the dealer. Likewise, no one purchasing a house or condominium wants to go through with the deal without at least trying to get a few thousand dollars knocked off the price, or some other concession. We haggle here at home, but only on the big items, which we buy only now and then.

Haggling is not just a quaint custom practiced by ignorant peasants who lack a pricing structure. It is a mechanism for determining the current, up-to-the-minute price of something of value. We've seen in Chapter 7 how the value of a seat on an airplane dwindles to almost nothing as takeoff time approaches. Or how a hotel room that's empty at 11 p.m. is worth a lot less than a hotel room that's empty at 11 a.m. A Third World merchant will haggle with you over the price of a cheap trinket or bauble. Why? He paid very little for it: you want it and you're willing to pay according to your value structure. He has to find out how badly you want it, and what your value structure will allow you to pay before he decides what to charge. So he bargains.

Of course, haggling is much more than a pricing mechanism. Throughout the world, it is a social custom as well. A businessman taking clients out to lunch, or on a round of golf, is doing the same thing as a Turkish carpet merchant who invites you into his shop for tea or coffee. Just as no good businessperson here at home would think of discussing an important deal nonstop over a conference table, no self-respecting merchant in a Middle Eastern bazaar would think of waiting for more than 60 seconds to ask, "Coffee, tea, or soda?" The difference is only one of scale.

HAGGLING SKILLS

Half the fun of being a shopkeeper is dealing with people. The social dimension is almost as important as the price-setting one. Therefore, you should train yourself to be patient, to enjoy chatting with shopkeepers, and to sharpen your bargaining skills. Time and patience are needed, but the payoff is an enjoyable experience, and a much lower price.

Although most of the bargaining you do will be abroad, you must keep your eyes open for opportunities when you travel at home. Just because you don't normally haggle over price for some items does not mean that the shopkeeper is unwilling to do so. For all you know, the person coming into the shop as you leave will use a few well-placed words and a keen assessment of the shopkeeper's situation to get a better price than you just paid.

Is Haggling Appropriate?

The first thing to do is to determine if haggling is appropriate. If the shop is very busy, it may not be good to haggle; perhaps you should return later, or pay the price asked. In some shops, usually the posh ones catering to the carriage trade, haggling is simply not done. After all, people go to these places to be ripped off in a genteel manner, so what's the point of haggling?

Haggling is something we do frequently here at home. No one in his right mind would waltz into an automobile dealership and agree to pay the very first price put to him by the dealer.

It's simple to determine if haggling is appropriate. Just begin: offer a decent price that's somewhat lower than the asked (or marked) price. If the shopkeeper won't bargain, he or she will tell you so right away: "I'm sorry, but the price is as marked." When you hear this, you should get the feeling that the vendor doesn't care if you walk out of the shop without buying. A firmness of manner, and a vague whiff of condescension, will tell you that a shopkeeper won't budge. Whatever the reason for not bargaining—the price is alrcady low, or it takes time, or it would "lower the tone" of the shop—your path is now clear. You buy, or you don't buy, at the price offered. No hard feelings.

Warming to the Task

On the other hand, if the shopkeeper budges, or
even pauses for a moment, you'll know that his or her
brain is whirring to digest the consequences of your
offer. ("Can I sell it for that and still make a decent
profit? How important is this sale to me? I've got to
pay the rent tomorrow! Actually, I like this object and
wouldn't mind having it hang around the shop for a
few more weeks. . . .") That pause is your signal that
haggling is possible, and that in almost every case
there will be accommodation, some searching for the
Point of Mutual Advantage. You're in.

Determining Price

I was once visiting my sister in Morocco. I wanted
some of the fine leather items being sold in Rabat's
tidy bazaar. After wandering through its streets for a
half hour, examining suitcases, handbags, and hassocks in various shops, asking prices, judging quality,
I finally settled on the shop of an excitable but sympathetic old gent. He wore a formal outfit (tails) and a
fez, spoke French as though he were firing a machine
gun, and seemed only partly in possession of his wits.
But he was indeed sympathetic, he stocked quality
goods, and he seemed to have the lowest prices.

At the end of 45 minutes, we had finished numerous
glasses of sweet mint tea, and had arrived at one final
lump-sum price for what I wanted: a large suitcase,
two handbags, two hassocks, various little purses and
trinkets. He was happy. I was happy.

I proudly took my purchase back to my sister's
house. When I told her what I had paid (that is, what a
good deal I had gotten), she was ready to shove me
into her car and go tearing right down to the bazzar.
"That thief! That bandit!" she cried, "He's robbed
you mercilessly! I won't let him get away with that!"

This is not what I wanted to hear. A man of the world, experienced haggler, who had once gotten the best of a master haggler in Istanbul's awesome Grand Bazaar—such talk from my sister was not good for my ego.

"Well, what would *you* have paid?" I asked her.

"Half of what you did, maybe a third," she replied in scorn.

"How was I to know?" I murmured weakly in self-defense.

How *does* one know what to pay? The best and surest way to know is to live there and to shop in the markets frequently. Then you know. But we don't live there, and we can't shop there frequently. The worry-free method is the one my wife uses: tell yourself what an item is worth to you, and then stick to your price. Say to yourself, "A leather suitcase at home would cost $200; this one is not as high in quality, but it's 'rustic,' and I like it. I'd pay $70 for it at home; I'll pay $35 or $40 for it here." Do all this thinking *before* you have any idea what the shopkeeper wants.

Haggling is not just a quaint custom practiced by ignorant peasants who lack a pricing structure. It is a mechanism for determining the current, up-to-the-minute price of something of value.

Your price is $35 or $40. You ask the shopkeeper. He says, "For you, because you're from (blank), and because you're my special friend, and because it is such a beautiful day, and because my uncle's cousin's nephew's wife just had a baby, $50." Now your course of action is clear: bargain him down to $40 at least, $35 preferably, even lower if possible.

If he says, "For you, (etc.), $200," you counter with "I will give you $35 for it and not a penny more, take it or leave it." Get out the money—in cash. If he hesitates, you're close, and if you can't get it for $37 you will get it for $40. If his eyes bulge, and his cheeks puff, and a boy runs to get him a glass of water, you know that your price was not reasonable to him. Too bad. It was a nice suitcase.

This method avoids the sort of disappointment I suffered in the bazaar in Rabat because you assume there is no fixed price; you learn some people may get lower prices, but you know what the item is worth to you, you know what you think is fair. You are satisfied because you are getting your money's worth.

The other method is to try and get the lowest price possible. This demands more skill, more patience, more time. The more time you can spend hanging around shops, talking with shopkeepers, quizzing other tourists, examining goods, the better you will understand the market and its price structure.

Driving a Hard Bargain

You're determined to get the best bargain you can. Good for you! Start by getting acquainted with the market as much as time will allow. Know the goods, their quality, now and then casually ask a price (but don't make a counter-offer, or you've begun bargaining).

Once you are acquainted with the market structure for the items you want to buy, choose the shop which appeals to you. Don't show too much enthusiasm for the items you want. In fact, *convince yourself* that you don't need them, that you could walk away empty-handed and completely happy. This is one of those biblical contradictions, similar to "The meek shall inherit the earth": the way to get it for the best price is not to want it at all.

Once you've looked over the items in the shop, and have chosen the ones you might buy, you're ready to begin talking prices in earnest. Ask the shopkeeper what he wants for all the items combined. Counter his offer with a price which is very good for you, but which is not an insult. *Be ready to buy at that price.* It is very impolite to begin serious bargaining and not to buy if the dealer meets your price. He may jump at your offer, in which case it was probably too high. Too bad. By ancient custom and by modern law, you've come to an agreement and you've made a contract, and you must go through with it. Thus, make your counter-offer something you can live with.

The haggling process after these opening bids have been stated is merely one of narrowing the gap. Reasons are given for each new bid: "If the leather were finer, I'd pay more, but as it is I'll go as far as $12." The shopkeeper replies, "But this leather is durable, it'll last a lifetime. I can't let it go for less than $17."

Next round: "How do I even know my wife will like it?"

"She probably will; this style is selling by the dozens these days."

"If she doesn't like it, it's useless to me. But I'll give you $14."

"If she doesn't like it, you can always give it as a gift. What about $16?"

Clinching the Deal

Now you must be patient and creative. Look for ingenious reasons, especially ones which allow both of you to save face.

"You know, my daughter would really like a purse like this, but I can't spend more than $14." By saying this, you're giving the shopkeeper the opportunity to be kindhearted to your daughter. He saves face, because he appears to be cutting the price out of generosity, not because the price was inflated in the first place.

"Okay, for your daughter then, $14. I hope she likes it."

Another tack is to let the shopkeeper do you a favor: "I have another candlestick just like this one, and the two would make a pair."

"Oh, well then, you must have this one. I think I can give it to you for what you offered."

This gives the shopkeeper a chance to save face by being nice to you. But watch out! The price will be written in granite, or even raised, if you say something like "In my collection of 5000 coins, this is the only one I don't have yet!" Your appeal should be one of sentiment, not of covetousness.

As in any dealing, the face-saving aspect can be as minor as a well-timed joke: you both chuckle, the tension is broken, the deal concluded. It can be an appeal to patriotism: "I wanted a nice souvenir of your beautiful city (or country)."

Don't belabor the point for only a few pennies. Price reductions decrease geometrically during haggling: that is, you'll save tens of hundreds of dollars at the outset, but at the very end, just before the deal is concluded, you'll be bargaining over mere fractions.

If You Can't Agree

It may be that you just can't bring yourself to meet the shopkeeper's price, or vice-versa. All appeals to sentiment have been exhausted. However, there is one last tactic you can use: walk out. The shopkeeper must assume when you walk out that he will never see you again, that the deal is off. If he was truly undecided as to price, he may come running after you: "Okay, $25 it is." You have the advantage here, because if he fails to run after you, you will know that the last price was solid. If you want the item at that last price, you can always return (in an hour or a day) and buy the item at that price. You save face by saying, "I really can't afford this, but it is so beautiful," or "I won't buy that sweater I wanted; I'm putting the money toward this." The pressure is on the shopkeeper when you walk out, for you can always return, but the shopkeeper cannot always go out and find you.

Payment

Having agreed on a price, you must agree on a form of payment. This can be of real significance. Having made a deal and given you a good price on an item, a shopkeeper may not be willing to let you pay by credit card, because he must pay a percentage of the deal to the credit card company. He may demand cash in local currency, or in dollars. Surprisingly, personal checks are often readily accepted in foreign countries. The shopkeeper may require that you make it out to "Cash." In many areas of the world, your check will then pass between a hundred thumbs and forefingers, almost as though it were cash, before ending up in your check file at home.

Form of payment can be a bargaining point. Nothing speaks louder to a shopkeeper who has bills to pay than crisp banknotes crackling in your hand. Don't hand them over until the deal is clinched, though.

WHERE TO GET THE BEST PRICE

There is no real fixed price for any item in this world. A cigarette lighter which costs $5 in a discount store may cost $15 in a posh shop on New York's Fifth Avenue. When you are out shopping, at home or abroad, always keep in mind that location, style, clientele, overhead, supply, and many other factors that affect the store will affect the prices it charges.

Unfortunately, there are no easy, set rules to help you determine where to buy. It used to be that crafts sold in villages where they were made would be cheaper than crafts shipped to the big city and sold right under the tourists' noses. But craft cooperatives, very popular in countries such as Mexico and Guatemala, may now set prices by sophisticated marketing theories. You may actually find the same crafts cheaper in big cities due to the volume of business there.

In general, fixed-location shops are most expensive. If they don't sell an item one day, the proprietor can switch off the lights, lock the doors, and go home. The item will be there tomorrow, and so will new customers.

Open markets are less expensive, particularly late in the day, because a merchant here must pack up his goods and carry them if he can't sell them. Have you ever bought fish from an open-air market late in the day? They almost give it away. It won't last, and the merchant doesn't want to bother storing it. It's yours for pennies, though it sold for $5 a pound a few hours before.

Street vendors offer excellent bargains if they are authentic. If Señor Gomez decides he could use some extra cash, and if he gathers some Guatemalan Momostenango blankets on consignment, and takes the bus from Momostenango to Quezaltenango to hawk his beautiful blankets in the city park, you've got a dealer willing to give you a good price. But if Señor Gomez lives in Quezaltenango, and leaves home each morning with an armload of blankets, and returns home with the unsold lot each evening, then he's actually a merchant without a shop. Coming in from the village, a vendor doesn't want to return with unsold goods. But living in the city, a vendor may not mind returning with unsold goods; he'll just head out again tomorrow. If Señor Gomez is always in evidence, speaks English, and is up-to-the-minute on exchange rates, you've got a businessman, not a vendor from the village. And this businessman has no shop to which you can return with defective goods, no address to which the Tourist Police can accompany you. He may offer you a good price nonetheless. Fine, take it. But *caveat emptor:* know your goods, and check his stock very carefully before you buy.

DUTY-FREE SHOPS

Often you will hear the modern travelers' lament: "Duty-free goods used to be so cheap! Now those duty-free shops in airports are a rip-off." Is it true?

The question is, cheap for whom? You can get a decent bottle of cognac in the United States for $15. In London you will pay $25 or $30 for the same bottle. Thus, if the bottle costs $20 in a duty-free shop, it's cheap to a Londoner, but expensive to you.

Living in the midst of the world's largest market for consumer goods, Americans enjoy "volume discounts" on just about everything. On some "luxury" items such as liquor and tobacco, federal taxes haven't been raised significantly in 20 years, even though inflation has rendered the old tax rates ridiculously low. There is talk now of raising the taxes on luxury items, but until this is done, a "duty-free" purchase probably won't save you much over the normal U.S. price.

The whole rationale for duty-free shops has changed. They were first established to take advantage of "international waters." Ships that sailed out beyond territorial waters were subject to international maritime law, which imposed no luxury taxes nor forbade such things as gambling. Liners would stock luxury goods, make an agreement with national tax officials that the goods would not be opened or used within the national boundaries, and be exempted from national taxes. It was a service to passengers on which the ships might make a modest profit, or at least cover expenses.

The airlines got into the act, though there was less

rationale than with the ships. On a five-day crossing,
one might conceivably use up goodly quantities of
luxury goods; but how many cigarettes can you
smoke, how much whiskey can you drink, how much
perfume can you use on a six-hour flight? Still, it was a
service to passengers, and an airline might lose passengers if it did not offer this service.

Now, with huge shopping centers in every airport,
the duty-free shop has become not a place to save
money, but a place to spend time between planes, or to
buy last-minute gifts. You may save a few dollars by
buying in a duty-free shop, but only if you know prices
at home to compare. What did you last pay for that
bottle of scotch, or perfume? What price will your
local photo shop give you on a Nikon, or Canon, or
Minolta? Duty-free shops are not places to do casual
shopping. To get any good deal at all, you must be
prepared, and careful.

The Exceptions

Of course there are exceptions, places where duty-
free goods are ridiculously cheap. Most of these places
are islands (some Caribbean islands, the Canary Islands, etc.), and they use duty-free status to lure
tourists. There is Mutual Advantage here: they give up
a little something in the way of taxes, but duty-free
status helps convince tourists to spend the extra
money for the longer flight, and to spend a few more
days in local hotels, because tourists save significant
sums on luxury items. Not bad.

Another exception is this. You like to have a drink
before dinner, you've heard that your favorite drink is
very expensive in Europe, and you'd like to have your
own bottle. You didn't buy one at home (for $8), so
you pick one up in the duty-free shop (for $10) because
in Europe you've heard it costs $15.

Duty-free shops cater to one-way shoppers. No one

goes to the airport, shops by comparing prices, and then returns home, ready to take advantage of a better price at a local shop. By definition, *you have to be going somewhere*, leaving the country, to use a duty-free shop. Comparison-shopping is difficult. They know this. You keep it in mind, too. By the time you see their price, it's too late to go back into town and buy it for less.

Among the airports, Schipol in Amsterdam tends to be the least expensive, with many true bargains. London's Heathrow and Gatwick are about the most expensive. Why is this so? Well, the Dutch government wants people to use Schipol and to visit Holland, so they draw them with duty-free bargains. London, on the other hand, is the hub of the air-traffic world. The sheer mass of passengers filing through London's duty-free shops guarantees lots of business.

Tell yourself what an item is worth to you, and then stick to your price. . . . Get out the money—in cash. If he hesitates you're close. . . . If his eyes bulge, and his cheeks puff, and a boy runs to get him a glass of water, you know that your price was not reasonable to him.

What about on airplanes? In general, prices are pretty good on planes flying international routes. Airlines are not in the liquor, cigarette, and perfume retailing business (as duty-free shops are), and they'd rather not trundle the stuff around if they can't sell it. So they charge decent prices and look upon the sales as a service to passengers.

GETTING YOUR PURCHASES HOME

Nothing you've bought abroad does you much good if it never makes it out of Cairo, or Tel Aviv, or New Delhi. And all that wonderful haggling you did will seem as nothing if U.S. Customs hits you with an enormous import fee. Believe it or not, big discounts are available through the bureaucratic machinery which oversees international movements of goods. You can save twice, because you will have to deal with two sets of customs regulations, the first in the country you're leaving, and the second when you get home.

Getting yourself out of a country is usually no problem, but taking certain items out of a country can be difficult. Antiquities, works of art, precious items which represent a significant transfer of wealth across borders—things like this, if discovered in your luggage, can cause problems. You may be delayed, or you may have to pay a fine, or the goods may be seized.

Foreign Tax Rebates

Most of us aren't bringing home Greek statues, or antique icons, or old carpets, or uncut diamonds. Rather, we will have bought tweeds in Britain, leather goods in Jerusalem, glassware in Venice, pottery in Mexico. Many countries in the world levy a Value Added Tax (VAT) on consumer purchases. The rationale is that any item goes through several stages in its progress from raw material to finished product, and that at every stage value is added to the item. The tax, then, is levied at every stage at which the "value" is added. So much for accountants' legerdemain. What the VAT amounts to is a super sales tax, often of 10%, 12%, or even 15% or 20%, levied on the final purchase price of most items (food, medicines, and some clothing are often excluded). To encourage foreigners to shop in their countries, many governments that levy a

VAT also set up schemes whereby foreign visitors can claim reimbursement for VAT if they export the items they have purchased. Here's an example:

I go to Edinburgh, and I see a nice Harris tweed jacket. I'd like to buy it, but it costs about 8% more in Edinburgh than it does at home in Boston, where I live. Well, the British government is willing to reimburse me for payment of VAT (15%) if I take the jacket out of the country and "consume" it elsewhere. (Obviously, if they simply knocked off the VAT at the time of sale, I'd buy the jacket and then sell it to Jack McCoy, my Scottish friend, tax-free. The government would be cheated out of the tax.) First, I must make sure the store participates in the VAT reimbursement plan and I then tell the shopkeeper I'm going to take the jacket out of the country, and that I'd like forms to fill out for VAT reimbursement. I pay full price for the jacket, including VAT, to the shopkeeper. At the airport I show the forms and the jacket to the customs officer before I board my plane. I give the forms to the customs officer who signs (testifying that the jacket has indeed been exported) and mails them first to the customs office and then to the shopkeeper who sold me the jacket. The shopkeeper is exempted from paying VAT on my purchase; instead, he mails me a check for the amount of the VAT: 15% of the price I paid.

With such a scheme, the jacket which would have cost 8% more than at home ends up costing 7% less.

Complicated? Well, it was thought up by a government bureaucracy. Slow? Yes. But it does work, and it does provide you with substantial discounts. Who offers it? Not all countries, and not all shops. And the shops that participate do not always announce the fact in foot-high letters in their front windows. Most of them would rather not put up with all the paperwork, though they will do it if they think it will get them a sale.

Therefore, if you are in a country that levies a VAT, and that has VAT rebate plans, *you must ask* in a shop (preferably before you buy) if they can get you the VAT rebate. When you've done all that's required for your rebate, don't hold your breath waiting for the check. It may take months. But it will come.

U.S. Customs and the GSP

The second customs hurdle comes when you return home. The U.S. Customs officer at the airport or border crossing it is empowered to enforce a complicated body of regulations imposing duties (taxes) on various goods brought into the country. These taxes are aimed at the wholesale, commercial importer, and are meant to be an important source of revenue for the federal government. (Customs duties are among the most ancient forms of taxation.)

You may not be a commercial dealer, but the goods you bring in may have to be taxed as though you are. The government does grant exemptions from the customs duties, so let's look at those.

First and most familiar is the "personal exemption" which allows U.S. residents to bring in up to $300 worth of goods bought abroad without paying any customs duties whatsoever. Then there are the special exemptions on luxury items: liquor, tobacco products, perfume, jewelry. Here, you can bring in certain small quantities without paying duty.

Customs regulations are extremely complex, and unless you are a specialist you will simply depend on the customs officer to determine the amount of duty you owe. For instance, he will discover from his computer screen that cigarette tobacco is taxed at a low rate, but cigarettes themselves are taxed quite high; normal table wines are taxed at one rate, fortified wines such as sherry and port are taxed at another, sparkling wines at yet another. There is little for you to do at this point but wait, then pay.

You can save money if you plan your souvenir purchasing ahead, however. Customs, in its wisdom, has established what's known as the GSP (Generalized System of Preferences), special regulations which exclude certain goods from certain countries from being subject to duties. The GSP is actually a bit of foreign aid to various developing countries. Industries in these countries which do not compete directly or seriously with our own are encouraged by granting their products duty-free status. Thus, most ceramic ware you buy in Mexico—even if you buy $1000 worth—will come into the U.S. free of customs duties. Baskets from Guatemala will likewise be duty-free, as will guitars. Duty-free items change from country to country, and you will have to ask customs (or a U.S. consulate abroad) if a certain item from a certain country is free from duties.

What this all means is that you may be able to buy $500, $600, or even $1000 worth of goods abroad, and bring them all into the country duty-free. If you have $500 of GSP items, and $400 of dutiable items, you will end up paying duty on only $100 worth of goods (remember, you get $300 worth of goods in free under your personal exemption). The customs officer will apply the $100 to those items on which duty is the lowest.

One last note on customs. Imagine that you are a customs officer at a U.S. port of entry. Every day you deal with hundreds of people returning from abroad; every day you inspect suitcases being brought in from the Middle East, Africa, South America, Europe, the Orient. After a while, you know all the stories, all the pained expressions, all the nervous laughs, all the tricks. You can predict in two seconds what a person may have in that suitcase. Now, as a returning tourist, is this the sort of person you want to try and fool?

Shipping

Getting your goods home can be expensive and troublesome. Friends of mine recently traveled to India. They bought a rug, and wisely made arrangements to have it shipped C.O.D. Obviously, they weren't about to pay a substantial sum to a man in India, then fly home and wait for the rug to arrive. It might never do so. So the dealer proposed an ingenious solution. "I will ship it in care of your bank," he said, "with instructions that it be released only after the bank has received your authorization to transfer payment to me." Wonderful, fine, let's do it.

The problem was this: the Indian dealer did not know that in the U.S. there are different types of banks (merchant, commercial, savings, savings and loan, etc.) and that a savings bank—such as my friends patronized—could not by law perform commercial-bank transactions, like dealing with international rug payments. So the rug sat in customs while everyone spent lots of time working out a solution.

This is not the first time that international shipment of goods has caused expensive and time-consuming problems. In fact, international shipment very often seems to cause problems. You can avoid them, though.

Take things with you. If you simply can't (as with the rug), try your best to have them shipped with you on the *same plane*. If this is impossible, arrange to have them shipped so as to arrive at the U.S. point of entry *when you do*; or to have them arrive a day or two earlier. By following these suggestions, you can limit the number of people and procedures and locations involved in a shipment, and thus hold down the possibilities of complicated screw-ups. Air freight costs more than sea freight for large items; but sea freight charges are usually subject to a minimum, so that shipping 50 pounds costs about the same as shipping

500 pounds. Thus, air freight may not cost any more than the slower sea freight, and you can arrange to pick up your item and guide it through customs at the airport when you re-enter the country. And by dealing with your items yourself, you avoid the costs of a customs broker.

Where to Buy What

Local goods are cheapest. But of course, that's obvious. Or is it?

You are in Florence, and you've just seen Michaelangelo's magnificent *David*. You'd like a copy of it, however primitive, for a friend at home. Right outside, a street vendor has dozens of small copies. Every single one has been made in Taiwan.

It is not at all easy these days to determine which goods are local and which are transported or imported. But ever since I learned that the Stetson hat company was founded in Pennsylvania, and that hula skirts were exported from Britain, I've wondered about "local goods." What about the time I tried to buy V.S.O.P. cognac in a small town in France? "Where do you think you are," sniffed the woman behind the counter, "London, or New York? You may find it in Paris, but it will be expensive. Wait until you get home—it's cheaper!" French tax laws, and export pressures, do indeed make cognac cheaper to buy in New York than in Paris!

It's fun to shop in the local equivalent of a 5 & 10¢ store or a department store—you'll get more insights into a nation's lifestyle than you'd find in an armload of sociology textbooks, plus substantial savings on the kind of merchandise sold only in overpriced specialty shops back home.

What you should do is look beyond the obvious. For instance, I got a nice, useful, inexpensive souvenir of Cairo by seeking out the shops where local people shopped. Instead of looking at jewelry in Khan Khalili (which is what most visitors do), I went around the corner to a local caftan shop. A lady was bargaining vigorously with the shopkeeper and, having learned the numbers from one to ten in Arabic, I could understand enough to know roughly what she was paying for it. I tried one on (good as a nightshirt), and when the shopkeeper tried to charge me four times as much, I indicated that I had overheard what that local lady paid. I got my price.

14

Avoiding and Solving Problems to Save Time and Money

The joy and excitement of traveling in strange places can turn to misery when problems arise. Where do you find a doctor? What do you do if your wallet is lost or stolen? How do you react when a foreign official demands that you pay a bribe? Besides misery, you can be in for a good deal of expense. Accidents and mishaps cannot be avoided. But some problems can be anticipated, and you can prepare yourself to deal with them quickly and inexpensively. Get into training to deal with crises by reading over the following pages, which examine the most common travel problems and ways to make them go away.

MONEY PROBLEMS

Money matters take up more of your time while traveling than they do at home. Also, you've got your money-handling problems worked out at home: the supermarket will take your personal check, the gas station will take your credit card, the bank will provide you with cash at any time of the day or night from its computerized teller machine.

Handling money abroad can be very expensive, which is why money matters are an appropriate subject for this book. For instance, in some countries—including several in Europe—banks may charge you up to 3% to change your money. That means you give the foreign exchange teller in the bank $100 in U.S. dollars, and you get back $97 in local currency!

The same thing happens when you change local currency back into dollars as you leave the country. Thus, on at least part of your money you've paid the bank 6%!

Exchange Rates

The exchange rates quoted in the daily newspapers may not be the ones applied to tourist transactions. The *New York Times,* for example, lists the rates applicable for exchanges between commercial banks for amounts of $100,000 or more. Naturally, the bank will not give you such a preferential rate if you are only changing $100. But the commercial rate is still a good approximation of the rate you'll get.

In some countries, rates vary considerably from bank to bank and from bank to hotel or travel agency or money-changer. Look at it this way: you are selling a commodity (the dollars or other currency you hold) and you want to get the best price for it. If one bank offers you 5.54 French francs for it, and another bank offers you 5.61 francs, you sell to the latter and get more francs for your dollar.

I wish it were always as simple as going from bank to bank looking for the best rate. But it's not. Many banks give a better rate for travelers checks than for cash. Most charge a fee for the transaction, and the fee may differ from one bank to the next. The black market may offer much better rates of exchange, and may be perfectly safe—or perilously unsafe.

The fastest international transfers are made by telegraph. . . . The slowest way to get money is to wait for a personal check to clear through international banking channels. You must have lots of time for this—six weeks or more—and hitches and problems can develop.

What I can say here is that you must shop around, and you must always be aware of the *actual amount of cash which ends up in your hand*. In Jerusalem, you can exchange dollars for Israeli shekels at banks (both Palestinian and Israeli) or at money-changers. The money-changers, a colorful medieval holdout, are grouped around Damascus Gate. Transactions are very simple: no forms to fill out, no route through several tellers and cashiers to follow. The man or woman behind the counter pulls open a drawer and pays out cash for the money you've put down. The rate of exchange is not as good as at the bank. *But there is no fee*. If you are changing $1000, you may do better at a bank, for the fee is a small set amount which may equal only 1/10th or 1/20th percent of $1,000. But for amounts around $100, you do better at the money-changers, for the fee at the bank may be 1% or 2% of $100. Thus, at a money-changer, you walk away with more cash in your hand. In Jerusalem, this is all perfectly legal.

The Black Market

In many countries, black market currency transactions are punishable by long sentences in jail and large fines; in some countries these punishments are even meted out. But in others the black market is accepted as a fact of life, and participants are rarely prosecuted.

It's a tempting prospect, but look at it this way. It's true that if there is black market activity, then black marketing can be done and people do it daily without getting caught. But they're familiar with the local scene, and you're not. Just because you are approached on the street by someone who whispers "Change money?" in passing doesn't mean that's the way it's done. Could you tell a plainclothes police officer from the dealer? Do you know whether exchange transactions can be safely carried out in public places in broad daylight? In the final analysis, don't do it—change your money at a bank or money-changer where you'll still get a good rate—and safe exchange.

Emergency Funds

If you run out of money you pay a hefty price. You will have to spend priceless vacation time standing in lines at banks and telegraph offices. You will probably have to stay in one place longer than you desired. You will have to pay for telegrams, telephone calls, bank fees, etc. You may have to change hotel and transportation reservations. It's terrible.

For American citizens abroad, there is a quick way to handle money emergencies with the help of the nearest American consulate. Call your family (or friends) back home and ask them to draft a Western Union money order payable to the Department of State, and a telegram with your full name, the exact district of the overseas consular office, and the sender's full name and address. This should be sent to the Department of State, Citizens Emergency Center, Room 4811, 2201 C St., N.W., Washington, DC 20520 (tel. 202/632-5225, weekdays 8:15 a.m. to midnight; for after-hours emergencies, 202/655-4000). The Department of State must receive payment before you can receive any money at the consular office. The transaction takes about 24 hours once the money order has been sent to Washington.

CASH FROM YOUR CREDIT CARD: If you have a major credit card, and if you are careful always to have some credit available on it, there's no reason you should want for money either at home or abroad. Without such a card, good planning can often avoid money crises; if you see that you're about to run out of money, act immediately to get more. Here are various methods:

MONEY BY TELEGRAPH: The fastest international transfers are made by telegraph. Sometimes the telegraph office acts as a transfer bank (this is true in countries where the post office, telephones, and telegraph are operated by the government; the post office is usually a savings bank as well). You go to the telegraph office with your passport (for identification), ask them to wire your bank with an order to pay you a certain amount, and then wait for it all to come true. It may take hours, it may take weeks. Several days is the usual time. The telegraph office may have to work through several banks. For instance, if your account is in a savings bank, that bank will have to apply to a commercial or merchant bank for help since savings banks don't normally engage in such transactions. All this takes time, and each bank—as well as the telegraph office—will charge you for its time.

BANK TRANSFERS: Plan ahead, and you can save lots of time and money. Just write a letter to your bank asking them to transfer a certain amount to a certain bank (and branch) abroad. If you don't know a bank, just walk into one and ask if they will be able to accept the transaction. But what if you're in Budapest, and you want the money delivered in Stockholm? Then tell your bank this, and give them an address in Stockholm (Poste Restante will do) where they can reach you. When you get to Stockholm, go to the Poste Restante and pick up the bank's reply, which will contain the name of the bank to which the transfer has been sent. Go to the bank with your passport and the bank's letter, and pick up your money.

THE SLOWEST WAY: The slowest way to get money is to wait for a personal check to clear through international banking channels. You must have lots of time for this—six weeks or more—and hitches or problems can easily develop.

OFFICIAL HELP: "Well, I can always cash a personal check at the U.S. consulate." Wrong. The embassy or consulate will not accept your check—personal or travelers—and will not lend you money. People in dire circumstances have been helped by their fellow citizens, but this is a private effort. Diplomatic personnel will sometimes chip in to a charity fund to be used for the relief of Americans who run into problems abroad. This is definitely charity, though.

What about those stories of people who ran out of money and were flown home at government expense? This does happen. Here's how: you apply for repatriation at a consulate, and if you are accepted, you turn in your passport and agree to *pay back the loan* (with interest) which the government will make to you in the form of a commercial airline ticket. When you pay back the loan, you get your passport back—not before. Other security may be demanded as well. It's no fun.

Losses and Thefts

The chilling moment comes when your purse or wallet is not there where it should be. You've forgotten it somewhere, or it's been stolen. In either case, you have a chance to get it back.

Retrace your steps. Ask as many people as possible. Mention where you're staying, so they can notify you if it turns up. If you think it's been stolen, check in wastebaskets, bushes, gutters—a thief doesn't want the evidence of the crime on his person, and after extracting your cash and travelers checks he may dump the item quickly. Notify the public officials nearby of the loss: subway or bus people (they always have a special lost-and-found office), policemen on the beat (if they still exist), even street sweepers if you see them. Tell them your name and where you're staying, always. About half the time, something comes back to you—the empty wallet, or wallet and personal items, or maybe even credit cards. About 10% of the time you get your money back, too!

REPORT THE LOSS: You will probably suffer some permanent loss, monetary or personal, if your wallet or purse disappears. Report it to the police, get a copy of the report (or at least a summary or note), and make a claim against your traveler's or homeowner's insurance when you return home. Yes! Homeowner's insurance will cover many such losses.

For lost travelers checks, you apply to the issuing bank or its representative. You will need your passport, and perhaps the police report of the loss.

MEDICAL AND HEALTH PROBLEMS

Nothing is quite as scary as getting sick when you're far from home. Besides the uncertainty of "What's wrong with me?" there is the problem of whom to consult. Where is the doctor? When can I get an appointment? Will there be a language problem? How much will all this cost? See Chapter 5 under "Medical Matters" for some tips on reference books to consult before you leave. But if you're suddenly taken ill:

Finding an English-Speaking Doctor

Contact your embassy or consulate for the name of a recommended local physician who speaks English. The consulate won't guarantee good service; but any doctor, hospital, or clinic that occasions complaints is removed from the list. A diplomatic duty officer is on call even when the consulate or embassy is closed. The number may be in the telephone book; in some cases, it's posted on the door of the consulate building, and you may have to send someone to go look for it.

Your hotel may also be able to provide the names of doctors and clinics with which you can deal in English, and which have proved satisfactory.

In an emergency, remember: most hotels have doctors on call; that taxis are a cheaper, and many times faster means of reaching a hospital than ambulances; that as a general rule, public hospitals abroad have 24-hour service, a larger range of facilities, and better-trained staffs than do private ones.

Be warned that payment for medical treatment abroad must nearly always be made by you directly to the doctor or hospital. Make sure that you obtain itemized statements for your insurance company.

Dental Care

The same rules apply for finding a dentist: check with the local consulate. Dental practices vary somewhat from country to country, but you needn't fear that you will have to settle for the sidewalk dentist in the bazaar of Fez who sits you on a stool, takes an ordinary pair of pliers, and extracts the tooth with a violent jerk. On a plastic sheet set out in front of him are the dental relics of all his former patients. Some of these unfortunate souls may still be alive!

"Well, I can always cash a personal check at the U.S. consulate." Wrong. The embassy or consulate will not accept your check—personal or travelers—and will not lend you money.

Rather, you are more likely to run into a dentist trained in the United States or Europe. In Istanbul, I had dental work done by a man who attended the same college I did. We spent half the time chatting about professors, football seasons, and the yacht club.

Eyeglasses

If you've brought your prescription with you, it should be fairly simple to get replacement glasses. Any major city will have a well-equipped and modern optometrist's shop. It may be expensive.

Contact lenses are not so easy to find, however. You may have to arrange for them to be sent from home.

AIR TRAVEL PROBLEMS

Lost Airline Tickets

What if you lose the return portion of a round-trip airline ticket? A simple matter to replace it by checking with the airline computer? *Not* if you don't have the number of the original ticket! Most likely, you'll be required to purchase another return ticket, sometimes at prices higher than the initial cost. A simple precautionary measure is to record the number of your round-trip ticket right along with your passport number and travelers checks information and tuck it away in a safe place. With the ticket number, the computer goes into action and your ticket can be reissued in little or no time. No expensive repurchase or layover days waiting for records to be checked.

Do complaints help? Yes. An unqualified yes. They always help.

Baggage

Just when we thought we had baggage allowances down pat, some of the airlines are looking at the whole question of checked and carry-on bags and tightening or changing existing regulations. Most major lines still adhere to the dimensions rule—free checking of two pieces of 62 and 55 inches (the sum of the length, width, and height of each case) and one carry-on of 45 inches, which will fit under the seat. Excess baggage charges vary widely from line to line. *Always* check with your reservations agent for current allowances. There may have been a change since your last flight!

What happens if your luggage is lost? Well, first of all, let's talk about some things you can do to prevent that kind of disaster. There is, of course, the obligatory identification tag which all airlines require on each piece of luggage, whether checked or carry-on. Tags are available at no charge at all airport check-in desks. Before affixing a new tag, *be sure to remove all old destination labels*—otherwise, some harried baggage handler may send your suitcases back to where you've already been instead of where you're headed. It's a good idea, too, to supplement the outside tags with some form of identification—a business card or label with your name and home address and telephone number—taped firmly to the inside of your bags. It will speed up their return enormously in case the outer tags are missing when your bags go astray.

There are a few simple precautions you can take at the check-in desk. First of all, ask the agent the code letters for your destination, then check to see if your bags have been marked correctly for destination and flight number. *Always* compare the stubs you're given to those on your bags to be sure they correspond. And above all, don't pack valuables or irreplaceable papers or medicines in luggage you plan to check—those should travel with you in carry-on bags.

Now, if in spite of everything, you wind up one place while your luggage takes off for parts unknown, proceed immediately to the airline desk to fill out the required claim form. Do this *before you leave the airport*. Give the most accurate description you can of each bag and its contents and insist on a copy of the form for your own records. The airlines have a pretty good record of tracing and returning lost baggage and have recently installed sophisticated computer systems to increase the speed with which you and your luggage will be reunited. Still, there are those cases when bags simply disappear. If that happens to you, you may be in for a six-week to three-month wait for compensation (carriers are under no time limit to settle a claim), and if you feel the reimbursement falls short of actual value, your only recourse is to sue in a small claims court.

For detailed information on how to deal with lost—or damaged—luggage, as well as a number of other airline emergencies, write for a helpful booklet called "Fly-Rights" which by rights should be part of your carry-on luggage on every flight. It's free from the Civil Aeronautics Board, 90 Church St., Room 1316, New York, NY 10007 (tel. 212/264-1700).

BORDER CROSSINGS AND BRIBES

The scene was Mexico's mountainous jungle state of Chiapas, on a sweltering hot summer day. I was approaching the Guatemalan border, my head filled with horror tales about the rapacity of Central American border officials. But I was prepared: my car was an immense Ford LTD station wagon, a used car to me but to Central Americans a sign of unequalled wealth and power. Dressed in a suit and tie, I donned a pair of intense black sunglasses. A scowl curled my lip. I was ready.

Everyone was respectful, deferential, polite, but still official. I paid the official $1 fee for DDT spraying of my car, and the official $1 fee for my Tourist Card. And that was all.

Several years later the scene was quite different. I approached the selfsame border station in a red VW minibus, dressed in a sport shirt and blue jeans, a smile brightening my countenance. The border officials took their time, scowled at me. I paid dearly for my pleasant attitude and informal appearance.

The point is this: not everyone pays bribes, and not everyone pays in the same amount or with the same frequency. What you want to do is to become part of the crowd that doesn't pay. Though Central American border officials do indeed have a well-earned reputation for rapacity, you can frequently get by them if you're prepared. Officials in other developing countries have similar mind-sets, and you can deal with them in the same manner.

Not everyone pays bribes, and not everyone pays in the same amount or with the same frequency. What you want to do is to become part of the crowd that doesn't pay.

First, look important, respectable, serious, and wealthy. I was able to wear a suit on that first venture into Guatemalan officialdom because the Ford had an arctic air conditioner. The VW did not, hence the necessity for less formal dress. In many situations it is impossible to dress formally, but at least one can look austere or sinister, perhaps by wearing light-weight black clothing. Sunglasses are a great help. Always scowl, say little, and affect an air of mild annoyance and impatience.

Be careful, though! Maintain an attitude of correctness and civility, and never raise your voice, get angry, or insult an official! Not only does this blow your cool, it threatens his dignity which, for most Third World officials, is worth more than the paltry official salary. If his dignity is threatened, he will be forced to take steps to protect it, such as not letting you enter the country (minimum) to tossing you in the slammer (maximum, to start).

A border official (customs officer, immigration officer, border patrol officer) will put the touch on you if you look pliable, gullible, friendly, or frightened. If, on the other hand, you stand your ground and allow him his dignity, he will usually let you through without paying. He doesn't want trouble, he wants easy money. If you look important—perhaps as though you have important friends in the capital city—he'll want to stay out of your way. Often the officials at airports will not hit you for bribes, as people who fly are assumed to be rich and important. And airports are places that specialize in speed, efficiency, the modern outlook. But at a highway or railroad border crossing or international wharf, thousands of simple local people will be crossing with you. Each of them will be made to pay a pittance. After so many pittances, you will look like King (or Queen) Croesus to an underpaid border official.

A textbook, real-life example of how to beat the high cost of bribery: the Mexican government maintains a commercial frontier between the Yucatan peninsula and the rest of Mexico. Commercial vehicles must stop here to have their cargoes and papers inspected. Tourists are also flagged down by the sole officer, and are asked to show their papers. One used to need two official papers to drive through Mexico: a Tourist Card and a Temporary Vehicle Import Permit. Later, these were merged into a single document, and there was some confusion for people used to having two papers.

The Yucatan frontier officer devised an ingenious scheme by which to earn extra cash. He exploited the confusion.

Like everyone else, at first I had assumed I lost one of my papers, or an official had neglected to return one to me. But I discovered in Mexico City that the single document I possessed was dual-purpose. So when I encountered the mercenary Yucatan frontier official, I felt sure of my ground.

"You must have two permits, Señor." he said.

"One, Señor," I answered. "It used to be two, but now it is one."

"I have always seen two; where is your other one?"

"I have no other one because it is no longer issued. If you read the one I have, you will see that it is sufficient." I was firm, but very polite.

"Well, how can I be sure. . . ?" He saw his bribe slipping away.

"I am certain, Señor. Thank you very much. Please excuse me. Goodbye."

I bowed politely and left. Later that day the official claimed $5 from a friend who drove through and who did not stand his ground.

Please, please make the distinction between official fees and bribes. An official fee or tax, no matter how silly, stupid, unfair, or rapacious, *must* be collected by an officer. Arguing with him over such a fee is useless. He'll tell you, in so many words, "go tell Congress." But if it is truly an official fee, you have a right to receive a receipt, and you should ask for one if it is not provided automatically. A bribe, on the other hand, is something he can collect or not collect as he likes.

FIGHTING BACK—COMPLAINTS

It would be wonderful if I could tell you that by following the advice of this book, you would avoid all

disappointing situations. Alas, the world is too complicated a place to avoid all bad times. But it is certainly
true that keen-eyed and clear-thinking travelers avoid
many unpleasant situations encountered by their less
aware fellow travelers.

It is not unusual for an emergency call
from a hotel in a foreign city to the U.S. to
cost upward of $100. Obviously, this is
outrageous.

Each year I receive hundreds of letters from readers
of my guidebooks detailing their travel experiences
both in the United States and Canada, and abroad.
Corresponding with readers is one of the most pleasur-
able and satisfying parts of my work, and also one of
the most informative. About 85% of the letters describe enormously satisfying and rewarding trips, with
perhaps one or two hitches along the way. Perhaps one
will say, "The Hotel Palace was fine, but the Restaurant Delicatesse must have a new chef—all the food
tasted as though it had been boiled for hours." Another 10% of the letters is devoted to one particular
travel experience which was upsetting: "the bus from
the capital to the ruins is woefully inadequate for the
crowds; the driver always overcharges; and it's always
several hours late—please warn your readers!" The
last 5% are the unfortunate people who have had a bad
trip, and who tend to blame all those connected with
it—airlines, hotels, restaurants, travel agents, and
guidebook writers—for the disaster.

Do complaints help? Yes. An unqualified yes. They
always help. They may not get you your money back,
and indeed you might not even be able to see direct

results from your complaint, but a complaint always registers. Eventually, action is taken.

If I get a complaint about any establishment mentioned in one of my books, I check it out extra carefully on my next inspection trip. I ask around and find out from others if there have been more complaints. If I receive two or three complaints, the establishment had better have some very redeeming features, or a change of heart, if it is to be included in the next edition of the book. More than three complaints, and I'm pretty sure the place is a loss, though I feel that out of fairness it must be reinspected with an impartial eye.

This is the concrete effect your complaint has on the opinion, and product, of a guidebook writer. Similar effects register with travel agents, local tourist boards or chambers of commerce, or governmental tourist authorities. Think of it this way: a complaint is a vote, a negative note. One vote alone means little, but the effect of many votes can be overwhelming. Sadly, one only learns about the "candidate" (a particular hotel, restaurant, etc.) after having experienced a bad time.

Why don't writers, managers, and officials pay even more attention to complaints? Why not just close a place down, or exclude it from publication, or blackball it, on the basis of a well-voiced complaint? If it could happen to one person, it could happen to a million. The reasons are that all complaints are not equal, and that conditions change frequently.

When a chef falls ill, or goes on vacation; when a hotel changes manager, or hires new staff; when equipment breaks down unexpectedly; when there are too many visitors for facilities to handle—this is often the time when things go wrong. Such situations are understandable, and sometimes excusable. But there are two sides to every story, and also to every complaint. The hotel manager may say, "I'm terribly sorry the water's off, but there's nothing we can do about it—

the city main burst." Still, it is disappointing to be cheated out of a shower after a long day of sightseeing. Or to dream of a romantic dinner, and find you're next to a huge table of birthday-party revellers.

Your bad experience can depend partly on your frame of mind. If you've saved and saved for years so you can fly off to Paris, stay at the Crillon, and dine at Maxim's, everything had better be perfect, completely perfect. When you have a wonderful memory of a city, or a restaurant, you want to return and have it be exactly the same. And if your standards of cleanliness and service are high, you may find it hard to understand that the best place in town is a dump. One week, I received two letters from readers describing their experiences at exactly the same hotel. "The place was so beautiful, the food was so interesting and delicious; the owner and his wife showed us everything in their own car!" The other letter said, "The room was dusty, there was grit in the halls, the dinky light bulbs left everything in perpetual near-darkness, and the owner could have cared less—he was never around!" Both of these descriptions are probably accurate.

This is not to suggest that you should not register your complaint. You should, you must. But if you think that your complaint is meeting with indifference, it may just be that the person to whom you complained is waiting for more evidence.

It matters greatly where you lodge your complaint. A reader once blamed me because her room did not have a view of the sea, and I had described the hotel as having "windows looking either onto the bay or the inn's lush grounds." Her request for a room with a sea view should have of course been lodged with the hotel reservations clerk. Or, upon arrival, she could have asked for such a room when she registered.

It also matters greatly *how* you lodge your complaint. A polite but firm request should be met with satisfaction or a reasonable excuse, and you have every right to expect such. But the person to whom you complain has every right to expect that you will be reasonable and polite. If you aren't, they will feel as though they have a right to ignore you. Besides, there are always those times when they are right and you are wrong. If you've lodged your complaint politely, you have nothing to regret.

Successful Complaints

Successful complaints, like wars, come about through a process of escalation. The rules of war will help you succeed:

Complain at once. Get satisfaction as soon as you notice something is wrong. Any time that passes works to the advantage of the other side: "The customer put up with it this long, it must not be important." When the waiter puts that unordered tray of delicacies on your table, or that expensive bottle of mineral water, speak up: "Excuse me, we didn't order this. Is it on the house? How much does it cost? Would you take it back, please?" Or when you notice your room is noisy, or the lock doesn't work, or there is no light bulb, bring these things to the attention of the front desk at once. Give them a chance to save face and make it right by fixing things or by giving you another room.

Be polite and civil, but firm and persistent. Do not shout or use threats. Rather than saying, "I'll report you to the manager!" if the waiter or desk clerk ignores your request, do just that—report him to the manager. Do it without the clerk's knowing, so he won't get to the manager first with excuses.

Be reasonable. Determine if the other side has a legitimate case. Service was slow at the restaurant, and you almost missed the first act at the opera? For the romantic couple lingering over each course in that dusky corner, service was probably too fast. Perhaps you should have mentioned to the waiter that you had to make an 8 o'clock curtain, and asked for his suggestion on how you might order. Or if that hotel in the jungle is too expensive for what it is, consider what it must be like to run a hotel in the jungle. The people who work at the hotel probably view it as the height of luxury. Perhaps they think it's silly to pay $20 (a fortune!) for a concrete-block room when one can sleep under a tree for nothing. That's when you must decide if it's worth it to pay $20 so you don't have to sleep under a tree.

The inflexible law of tipping is this: the person who importunes you the most will need the tip least. . . . Never allow yourself to be shamed into tipping or into tipping big.

If you've truly been cheated, join battle to win. Now you're sure it's not just a mistake, or an accident, or your bad mood, or some other person's bad mood. These people are out to get you, and that overcharge is premeditated and deliberate, or they have no intention of providing what they promised. Proceed quietly and deliberately. Set aside time to do it. Keep appealing to higher authority as necessary, from the waiter to the maître d' or hostess, from them to the manager or chef, from them to the tourism bureau or chamber of commerce, from them to the national authorities; to guidebooks, travel agents, newspapers. Let word get around. Persist.

Remember, complaints *always* help. I'd estimate that in 60% of the cases you'll get full and immediate satisfaction if you lodge your complaint according to the rules. The rest of the time, you will attain satisfaction eventually, or you will influence someone who will see to it that the wrong is made right.

Finally, don't rule out the use of humor to get what you want. A well-placed joke can defuse an antagonistic situation, melt a heart of stone, or make everyone see the lighter side of life. Make someone laugh, and they've got to like you. And if they like you, they'll do anything for you. Of course if they don't laugh, they probably deserve the bombardment you're about to unleash upon them.

Embassies and Consulates—What They Can Do

An embassy is the diplomatic representative of one government to another government. A consulate is charged with the welfare of its nations' citizens and business interests in a foreign city.

Embassies deal with governments, consulates deal with people and firms. Consular officers will do their best to see that you receive equitable treatment under the laws of the foreign country in which you find yourself. They can recommend lawyers, visit you in prison, petition the foreign authorities. But they cannot guarantee your safety, they cannot get you out of jail or out of the country, make travel arrangements, forward your mail, or act as a bank.

A consular offier will gladly renew your passport, advise you of customs regulations in the U.S., warn you of dangers in the country, or provide business materials dealing with the foreign country. You can register at a consulate abroad, and if there is trouble they will attempt to contact you and let you know.

DAILY CONCERNS

Everything that's so cheap and easy at home seems to turn into a chore when you're on the road. Famous Nobel laureates and people who rule vast commercial empires can turn to imbeciles when faced with a foreign pay telephone: how do you get the cursed thing to work? Where can I get my laundry done? What do you mean, it will take five days? Tips to cover these sorts of daily concerns could never solve all your problems. But the few selected hints mentioned below will probably come in handy to save you money.

Laundry

I always have supplies to do my own, just in case. Elaborate supplies can include a bottle of concentrated liquid detergent, a small string for a clothesline, aluminum or inflatable hangers for drip-dry shirts, a drain stopper for those budget hotel rooms which always seem to lack them, a small brush for getting out spots and stains. Simple supplies are just the bath soap found in the room, hangers from the closet, and a rolled-up sock to plug the drain.

In some cities, all this is unnecessary. Pull into any big shopping center and there will be a coin laundry complete with washers, dryers, and vending machines selling everything from detergent powders to fabric softeners to laundry bags. In foreign countries, coin laundries (laundromats, washeterias, whatever your favorite term) may be scarce, but good old hand laundries may be common. You may get a jolly *señora,* or a dignified Chinese man, or a bevy of dark maidens to do your laundry for a very reasonable sum, and perhaps even deliver the freshly ironed garments to your hotel. Conversely, there are many countries in which the laundry bill is higher than the value of the clothes. In Switzerland one can pay $20 to have two shirts and some underwear cleaned; in Israel, I paid $8 to have a $10 pair of blue jeans washed and ironed.

Your hotel will always be able to arrange for laundry and dry cleaning, and will almost always take a cut of the action. In most cases it's better to make your own arrangements. Ask at a café or query a taxi driver, and find the location of a nearby laundry. Even if you don't speak the language, even if the sign is in Arabic or Swahili, laundries are pretty much the same the world over. What changes is price and time. The clerk can write the price for you, and you can count out the day when it will be ready in sign language, or point to a calendar. Same goes for dry cleaning. But ask the price before you commit yourself.

Mail

Mail presents a dual problem: receiving letters and sending letters.

To receive mail, the most dependable way is probably through a branch of American Express. You must be a customer of that company (that is, you must hold their credit card, or use their travelers checks, or sign up for one of their tours), and there must be an Amex office in town.

Less dependable is Poste Restante (General Delivery). You will need your passport to collect your mail, and you may have to pay a small fee for each letter. In cities with more than one post office, your Poste Restante will be sent to the main or central post office unless addressed otherwise. You may have to apply for your mail at certain hours—don't assume you can pick it up anytime the post office is open.

In other countries Poste Restante is not as dependable as having your letter sent to a hotel. In Egypt, for instance, this is the case.

To send mail in foreign countries, do it in post offices. Hotel clerks may or may not know the proper postage for foreign letters. If they don't, it's not their letter that comes back, postage due—it's yours. Besides, hotels usually charge extra for their stamps, not to mention for their postcards. Often you'll find hordes of postcard sellers around the post office.

Remember that foreign post offices provide all the usual services: registered letters, special delivery (express), general delivery (poste restante), and money orders. These services may or may not apply to letters leaving the country; that is, if you pay for express service from Brazil to the U.S., the U.S. Postal Service will probably honor the special delivery provision. But a special delivery letter sent from the U.S. to Brazil may not be delivered extra quickly at that end.

Telephones

The major problem with telephones abroad is the cost of using them. In many countries, simple local calls are amazingly cheap—the equivalent of 5¢ or 8¢—but long-distance and international calls are fantastically expensive, costing several dollars per minute. In addition, most hotels add a surcharge if you call from your room or from a booth utilizing the hotel switchboard or operator. It is not unusual for an emergency call from a hotel in a foreign city to the U.S. to cost upward of $100. Obviously, this is outrageous. But how can you avoid it?

CALLING FROM A HOTEL: Try to avoid it. If you must, then first find out what a call will cost. Ask the hotel clerk, the English-speaking international operator, or a local person to estimate the charges. Ask the hotel about surcharges. If it appears as though the cost will be high, plan to reverse the charges. Have the call billed to your U.S. phone, or to the number you're calling. Sometimes you're allowed to do this, sometimes you're not.

A better way is to call home and briefly give the city, hotel name and number, your room number, and when you can be reached. Let the person then call you back from the U.S. and thus avoid the extra person-to-person cost and an exorbitant surcharge.

In Ireland, Israel, and Portugal, *all* hotels are members of **Teleplan**, which means they have agreed to limit their surcharge and will inform you how much the call will be. Elsewhere, these chains participate in Teleplan: Trust House Forte hotels in England, Golden Tulip in Holland, and Hilton and Marriott throughout the world.

PAY PHONES: First, a note about "taxiphones": in many countries you will find ingenious pay telephones called "taxiphones." The odd name comes from the phone's "meter," which automatically calculates time and distance for the call and charges you accordingly. The usual procedure is to approach one of these telephones (in a café, terminal, or hotel) with a pocketful of the sort of coins or tokens which the phone will accept. You load a quantity of coins into the phone, and they appear in a little glass chute. As you speak, the coins slowly drop, gone forever. When the chute is empty, the call is disconnected, so you must keep replenishing the supply of coins in the chute as you talk. Often there will be several chutes for the several sizes of coins.

Though taxiphones in some countries accept only small-denomination coins good for local calls (making it difficult to call long distance—how would you like to load 300 tiny 5¢ coins?), many in Europe accept high-value coins. In France, for instance, you can walk up to a phone booth on a Paris streetcorner, load in some coins, and dial a friend in the United States.

As for other types of pay phones, the rule is: don't insert your money until you're sure the phone won't work without it, as some phones are designed without coin-return provisions. If you get a dial tone, then dial. If it rings, let it ring. When the person answers, the phone may go dead, or you may hear blips—*that is the time* to insert the coin, or push the plunger, or whatever it seems requried to do, and not before. If you push in a coin before that point, it may be gone for good and you may get nothing in exchange.

Note that in some countries you pay for every second the receiver is off the hook—whether you get a busy signal, or an incomplete call, or an unknown number from the operator.

Telegrams and Telexes

The alternative to the telephone is the telegraph or telex. What's the difference? Well, a telegram can be sent to anyone, anywhere; but a telex can be sent only to someone with a telex machine (teleprinter). Telex machines are widely used in offices and hotels. In effect, they provide "written telephone service." One dials a number just like the phone, and when the other party answers, one types the desired message on the keyboard.

Telexes have a distinct advantage over the telegraph in terms of cost, though. With a telex, the operator can encode your message on tape beforehand, and when the call goes through to its recipient, the tape can be played at high speed, thus saving time on the line. Therefore, if you can send a telex, always do so in preference to a telegram. Don't know the telex number? Most telex offices have libraries of directories listing telex numbers for the entire world.

As for telegraph service, you can save money by requesting that your message be sent as a "Night Letter." This service is available in many countries. Your message is delayed only until the slack period for telegraph traffic arrives (sometime late at night). There is a maximum delay time, and if your message is still waiting to be sent at that time, it is sent whether traffic has abated or not. Night Letters give you more words for your money, and have a higher minimum word limit. This means that they are particularly good for longer messages. Your message may be only one line, in which case you might as well send it by normal service. When asking for Night Letter service, just write "NL" for the clerk if you can't speak his language—that seems to be the universally accepted abbreviation.

Tipping

This is always a problem in a strange society. Most of us feel that we should observe the customs of the country. We don't want to disappoint anyone, or insult them. At the same time, it's our hard-earned money that we're handing out, and we'd like very much to avoid giving more than is generous or necessary.

The inflexible law of tipping is this: the person who importunes you the most will need the tip least. The taxi driver who berates you for stinginess, the bellhop who scoffs at your proffered coin, the street beggar who asks for some larger coin, or two or three— they're on the take, and they're taking from you. They've seen that putting a tourist to shame can produce big money fast, and they're hooked on this source of income. Compare them to the quiet country man who is a guard at some remote archaeological site. Not often seeing tourists, he feels delighted and honored when you visit. He would not think of besmirching his hospitality by begging, unless he is in real need. And even if he truly needs some money, *you* may have to beg *him* to take it. In some cases, a small gift of something "foreign" (an American ballpoint pen or keychain, for instance), or a photograph or a postcard sent after you return home, will mean more to your newfound acquaintance than cash.

In any case, never allow yourself to be shamed into tipping, or into tipping big.

If you leave a tip on your dinnertable, or pay it into the hand of one of several helpers, who gets it? That's hard to say. The best policy is to pay each person directly if you truly want to express your gratitude. A restaurant in Istanbul used to employ the following rapacious tactic: a service charge was added to the bill, and you were expected to leave a tip on top of that. But this tip went only to the maître d' while the poor waiter got nothing. The tip was very important to the waiter as he was the lowest-paid member of the staff, and he would work hard to get it. How did he get his just returns? He stood by the door as you left, wishing you a good evening and hoping you'd figure out the unjust tipping system in time to give him a little something.

This system was close to robbery, but when one understood it, one knew to leave very little on the table, and a much larger amount in the hand of the waiter himself.

How much does one tip? This is the most difficult question of all. Many people think 15% is the minimum, and 20% the norm, especially when the pressures of operating in a foreign society produce fear and guilt. This fear and guilt may be costly, because local custom may dictate a tip of 3%.

I tend to think of 10% as the norm, 12% as good, 15% as tops. I think 20% is outrageous, and is in effect begging for love. In places where there is a service charge, no tip may be necessary; on the other hand, the service charge may go to the owner alone, and the staff may be expecting tips. Give something extra in this case, but not 10% or 15% extra.

What if you notice local people leaving only a few small coins on the table? Well, it may be that a small amount is sufficient—in Egypt, the equivalent of 65¢ will buy a workingman a bounteous repast of *fuul, taamia,* picked vegetables, tomato salad, fresh bread, hummus, and spring water—all he can eat. Or it might be that tipping is not an important matter, or is almost frowned upon, as in Switzerland and Israel. Wherever you go, you will encounter people who will want bigger and bigger tips. You will find them even in countries where tipping is not important. Why? Because previous travelers have tipped out of fear and guilt, and have corrupted the outlook of these service people. From wanting nothing, or very little, the waiters and cab drivers and guides want all they can get, and would gladly accept a tip of 100%. Why not? Tourists are giving money away, why not take it?

in ignorance of where he will be in approximately a week's time.

Actively involving the rest of your family in travel planning is absolutely necessary for a good trip. Be especially careful to do this if you are the take-command type. Delegate responsibilities, and then accept the results gracefully. It is not the actual trip which is important here, but each family member's mental picture of it. One cannot enjoy even the best vacation trip when forced to live in an eternal present jammed up against an inscrutable future.

Reducing Family Expenses

Traveling with children can be dauntingly expensive. All those restaurant meals—whether fully eaten or not—must be paid for, and if you want privacy at the end of the day, you'll need two hotel rooms, one for you and one for the children. The advantage you have as a family is bargaining power: the hotel, restaurant, or attraction you patronize is getting twice as much business, so they should be willing to give a discount.

TRANSPORTATION: Airlines have strict rules about who must pay, and how much, when it comes to children. There are family discounts, but they are not too exciting (except for the occasional super promotions—spouse goes free, children pay half fare, etc.). Airlines would just as soon try to attract singles or couples for those empty seats.

Trains are better, and family plans help here. Children tend to enjoy trains more than airplanes as there is more room to get up and stroll around, meet new people, and play with other children.

But a family's best bargain is a car. It costs little more to transport five or six than it does one. Whether it's your family car or a rental car, a private auto is the cost-effective way to go. It allows you to stop when

15

The Special Traveler

For many people, travel presents special problems and opportunities. What about women traveling alone? What about families traveling with children? What about single travelers, in a world set up to handle couples? These and other special situations can be turned to your advantage. Special strategies apply for saving money if you're not precisely the middle-class, middle-aged couple that the travel industry so often expects and equips itself to serve.

In this chapter you'll find information and suggestions for dealing with these special situations in a cost-effective way: first, youth and student travel, the Senior Citizen's travel, then families traveling with children. After dealing with family travel problems we'll look at ways to overcome the solo traveler's problems before taking a look at special interest vacations, from archeological digs to working on a kibbutz which leads naturally to the ultimate value of all—working abroad.

YOUTH AND STUDENT TRAVEL

When it comes to cost-effective travel, young people rule the road. Willing to take chances, to do without frills and comforts, and to forget considerations of rank and status, students can and do travel the farthest on the least. One reason for this is the vast network of youth hostels, student hotels and flights, discounts on ships and buses, inexpensive university cafeterias, even student travel bureaus.

A young person's passport into the worldwide network of student travel organizations is the International Student Identity Card, described in detail in Chapter 5. Once you're plugged into the network, you can get hold of the CIEE's *Student Work-Study-Travel Catalog*, and also the *Update* to the catalog which is mailed out later in the year when travel prices have solidifed.

A young person's passport into the worldwide network of student travel organizations and discounts is the International Student Identity Card.

The catalog is free. It contains a complete list of International Student Travel Conference (ISTC) offices abroad, information on books and guidebooks, an application form for the International Student Identity Card, and full information on student travel opportunities. An added feature of the catalog is a large section on "Work Abroad" in countries throughout the world. The CIEE has negotiated agreements with many countries which make it possible for students to work in foreign countries for limited periods without hassling over normal work permits (sometimes impossible for foreigners to obtain). Finally, the catalog deals in detail with opportunities for study abroad. Note that CIEE activities are of interest to high school as well as college students.

If you want even more information than the 64-page catalog provides, go to any bookstore and pick up the CIEE's *Whole World Handbook: A Guide to Study, Work & Travel Abroad* (New York: E. P. Dutton, 1981). The price is about $6, and for that you get over 300 pages of tips, addresses, directions, and opportunities. Note that the *Handbook* is no replacement for the aforementioned catalog and update, because it does not carry the same current information as do the smaller publications. The *Update*, for instance, is almost all totally full of charts of airfares for student flights. If you're traveling in the United States, get hold of a copy of CIEE's *Where to Stay U.S.A.*, available in bookstores. Make sure you contact the **Council on International Educational Exchange** at 205 East 42 St., New York, NY 10017 (tel. 212/661-1414).

For students who like to ski: contact the **Student Ski Association**, 26 Sagamore Rd., Seekonk, MA 02771, or 2256 North Clark St., Chicago, IL 60614.

SENIOR CITIZEN SAVINGS

The rationale for giving discounts to older people runs like this: "Here we have this large group of citizens who have come to enjoy the finer things in life, but who now are living on limited retirement incomes. They have the time and the inclination to travel, but perhaps not as much money as they'd like. Seniors represent a vast pool of customers for airlines, trains, buses, hotels, and restaurants. They're good customers, too: no vandalism, robberies, or bad times with seniors, by and large. The way to attract this large clientele is by offering discounts."

Well, that's the rationale. And it works, though senior discounts are sometimes small and sometimes cancelled when trade is brisk—the bright side is that you don't have to work hard to get them.

SENIOR CITIZENS' ORGANIZATIONS: First thing to do is to join a recognized senior citizens' organization. The dues are a small amount, and the benefits are substantial. Best-recognized is the **American Association of Retired Persons** (AARP), affiliated with the **National Retired Teachers Association**, 1909 K Street N.W., Washington, DC 20049 (tel. 202/872-4700); another big one is the **National Council of Senior Citizens** (NCSC), 1511 K Street N.W., Washington, DC 20049 (tel. 202/347-8800).

For senior citizens, the first thing to do is join a recognized senior citizens' organization. The dues are a small amount, and the benefits are substantial.

Why does it help to be a member? Because firms are much more likely to give discounts to members of a group that number in the tens of thousands, hoping to attract more and more members to their services. And seniors' organizations can negotiate with firms on that basis as well. Also, you can often slip in under the wire on discounts which are given out to "retired persons" (i.e., over 65) because you can join the AARP at age 55 and reap the benefits.

SENIOR DISCOUNTS: If you've followed the advice of this book and have sent away for the directories of the budget motel chains, you already have a head start on senior discounts. Many hotel, restaurant, and transportation firms require that you hold their own identification card or join their own seniors' club in order to get discounts, and the directories tell you how to get them. Often this costs nothing (or just a dollar or two). The entire procedure seems designed to get your loyalty: thinking that you won't bother to send away for the other chains' cards, and will only use theirs.

Be careful, and calculate exactly what you'll be getting with your senior discount, whether the deal is for a motel room, airfare, or train ticket. Stipulations will be made, such as that you must reserve one of the nicer (and pricier) rooms in order to get the 10% discount, or that you must fly on a certain flight, or pay in advance. All this may be fine, but you also may be able to do better by ignoring the senior discount and looking for normal cost-cutting deals as described in this book. For instance, if a hotel is offering a special weekend rate, that rate will usually be much better than the normal "rack rates" minus 10%. The same goes for transportation: if you must pay full fare to get the 10%, you may do better by signing up for an excursion or promotional fare.

> Be careful and calculate exactly what you'll be getting with your senior discount. . . . You may do better by ignoring the senior discount and looking for normal cost-cutting deals as described in this book.

Another stipulation often made is that one must arrange in advance to get the discount. You can't just pull off the highway at a chain motel (in some cases) and sign up for a room at a 10% discount. They want you to help them plan their workload by reserving in advance. In theory, that's the way it works. In practice, they won't turn you—or your request for the discount—down if they have the space and it looks as though it'll go unused.

An indispensable guide to senior discount possibilities is *The Discount Guide for Travelers Over 55*, by Caroline and Walter Weintz (New York: E. P. Dutton, 1981), a country-by-country, state-by-state, and even city-by-city guide to exact services and establishments that offer discounts to seniors.

The United States Golden Age Passport

The United States Government issues a Golden Age Passport to those 62 and over that entitles holders to enter all national Monuments and National Parks for free. Proof of age is required. For general information call 202/343-4747. State and city governments also offer a variety of discounts. Find out about them by checking with the local Office for the Aging or look up the number of the Senior Hot Line—most major cities have one.

The European Inter-Rail Senior Pass

All kinds of senior citizen discounts on transportation are available. In Europe one of the best, but *for European residents only,* is the Inter-Rail Senior Pass, which may be purchased in 17 countries for first- or second-class travel. It is valid for one month, and allows you to pay 50% of regular fare in the country of purchase, then ride free in all others. Obviously, it's best to buy it in a small country like Luxembourg. These passes can be purchased at any railroad ticket office (you'll need proof of at least six months' residency in a European country) in the participating countries: Austria, Switzerland, France, Germany,

Luxembourg, Belgium, the Netherlands, Greece, Portugal, Denmark, Sweden, Norway, Finland, Hungary, Yugoslavia, Roumania, and Spain.

Elderhostel

One exciting program offered to the over-60s is the remarkable Elderhostel program, which enables seniors to study at various colleges and universities throughout the U.S., Canada, Britain, and Scandinavia. Courses range from dance, literature, and art to astronomy, finance, ecology, and sociology. Although the courses are given year round, during the summer months more programs are offered and the costs may be a little lower because dorm accommodations are available. Prices from $150 to $180 a week (in 1982) cover room, board, tuition, and some extracurricular activities. To find out more about Elderhostel, contact the state and provincial offices nearest you (check your phone book, or information in the nearest large city), or write to Elderhostel, Suite 200, 100 Boylston St., Boston, MA 02116 (tel. 617/426-7788).

FAMILY TRAVEL

When I was in junior high school, my parents debated taking a vacation to Montreal and Quebec City. This was a great adventure for us, because as children we had always gone on vacation to the same lovely state park in Pennsylvania. My father charged me with gathering information for the trip, and started me off by pointing out the coupons attached to travel advertisements in magazines and newspapers. In no time I had a bulging file of maps, color brochures, French phrase books, historical walking tours, and technical explanations of the wondrous St. Lawrence Seaway. I loved it.

My father hated to be bothered with making travel plans. When he traveled, his corporation made all the plans and reservations. By "unloading" the vacation planning task on me, he made the vacation a child's adventure dream come true. What a stroke of luck that he hated planning! I can imagine how boring it would be for a child to be loaded into the car with no more idea about the destination than the strange word "Quebec." Endless miles of driving, hotels popping up from nowhere, unfamiliar food, other children who didn't speak my language. It could have been a disaster. Instead, it was a dream-come-true. As soon as I got home, I used my new-found capabilities as a travel planner to chart make-believe trips throughout the world, using those marvelous coupons which said, "Send for a free color brochure." Years later, I actually took many of the trips.

Actively involving the rest of your family in travel planning is absolutely necessary for a good trip.

Even adults can suffer from a powerful sense of being lost, in limbo, when they have had no active part in travel planning. If you're the one who has everything all mapped out, you may find it difficult to comprehend the problem. Showing others an itinerary may not be enough. They've got to be involved in the trip; it must mean something to them. There must be a mental panorama: tomorrow and the next day we'll be in Montreal, a city I know from travel folders and historical booklets; after that to Quebec City, which looks medieval and has quaint, winding streets and horse-drawn carriages. Not only must your family be able to picture the destinations, they must have a sense of where they will be, when. No one likes living

you want (or must), and to camp if you like. An even better choice would be a mobile camper (your own or a rental).

ACCOMMODATIONS: Every hotel and motel which features two double beds in a room should allow your children (teenage or younger) to stay for free. (Many extend the privilege to under-18s.) At most, they should charge only $5 or $10 extra. If they charge more, they have a reason for discouraging children as guests: perhaps the resort rate structure dictates that each bed must yield maximum income.

Most of the large hotel and motel organizations feature family plans which allow kids to stay in their parents' room for free. If your chosen hotel has no such policy, work one out with the clerk or manager. Unless the place is full, they will be willing to haggle. Often the best arrangement is to take a suite or junior suite at normal price (which is less than two normal double rooms) and have it set up to sleep all of you. Another arrangement is to get two double rooms for the price of two singles—you save a little money, and you get a lot more luxury. Remember: what you are trying to do is utilize hotel space that would otherwise go empty, because that's how you'll get a good price. What the hotel clerk is trying to do is get your business without giving up other business. He is used to making special arrangements for families (though you may not be used to it), and the suite-for-price-of-a-room or two-doubles-at-singles-price arrangements are just face-saving devices. In fact, he's simply dropping the price for you. If the hotel is not full, he'll be willing to do so. Remember that.

Families sometimes end up staying in the more luxurious hotels and motels for good reasons. They need extra convenience and the larger hotels tend to have better family services: baby sitters, bassinets and cribs, bottles and diapers.

OVERCOMING THE SOLO TRAVELER'S PROBLEMS

During the research for my guidebook on Turkey, I came across an old Victorian-era hotel in Istanbul. Prices were low, but so they should have been as the rooms were well worn and somewhat drab. Still, I gave the aged Hotel Bristol great play in my guide. Why? Because the Bristol, built to house British commercial travelers, had dozens of single rooms.

Except for YMCA's and prisons, no lodgings being built are designed to accommodate the single traveler. When it comes to air, rail, or bus tickets, entry to a museum or cinema, the single traveler does as well as anyone else. But in lodgings, and to a lesser extent in restaurants, the single traveler is at a distinct disadvantage.

There are two ways of looking at the lodging problem, as there are two ways of viewing a half-full glass of water. Just as the glass can be seen as either half-full or half-empty, a hotel room in a modern lodging establishment can be seen as underutilized if occupied by one, or super-efficiently utilized if occupied by two. Those faded single rooms at Istanbul's Hotel Bristol had *bathrooms* the size of today's standard-size hotel bedroom, so actual floor space has little to do with it. Rather, it is the hotel management's attitude that matters.

We've already studied some of these attitudes. One of them is "It costs us little more in the way of sheets, towels, water, and electricity to lodge two people instead of one, so the double price should be only a bit higher than the single price." Another is "We could lodge two people where that one person is staying, so the one person will have to pay almost as much as two—no sense losing that profit just because we agree to put up a single traveler."

Alas, all too often it is the second attitude that

prevails, and as a single traveler you can expect to meet with it. You enter the lobby, approach the desk, ask if there are any rooms, and the clerk answers your question with another question: "For one or two persons?" As there are hardly any one-person rooms in existence, the question really is an answer: "For two persons I have rooms; for one person, maybe not."

In a situation where rooms are in short supply, your battle is all uphill. Forget about getting discounts. The clerk hesitates even to give you a room, let alone a discount. Your attitude at this point should be the first of the two mentioned above, namely that the single-room price is very adequate compensation for the use of the room; the two-person price is gravy, and the hotel shouldn't demand it.

If they won't rent you a room at the single rate, try saying something like, "Then, I'm afraid I'll have to go elsewhere," and start walking away.

If they won't rent you a room at the single rate, try saying something like "Then, I'm afraid I'll have to go elsewhere" and start walking away. More often than not this will produce a quick reaction and a room for you at a fair price.

If the hotel is not busy, a single traveler has as much chance of getting a discount as a couple. Indeed, the whole idea of "commercial rates" was to give a break to the frequent, single business traveler. Some of the big hotel and motel chains have direct arrangements with big commercial firms regarding discounts: the firm's travel department books all company travelers into the chain's facilities at special rates. But most hotels and motels will take a chance that you're a commercial traveler (why else would you be traveling alone?) and that you'll come back again. So look like you're there on business, and then ask for a commercial discount. They'll ask what company you work for. They'll also probably ask for an ID. Your company identification card or a business card of some kind should do the trick.

Avoiding the Single Supplement

Although it seems very unfair to penalize the single traveler, it is done, and only by taking action yourself can you hope to avoid paying a single supplement on such items as package tours. When booking a tour, if you're willing to share with another single, always ask the tour operator (or have your travel agent ask the tour operator) to match you up with another solo traveler. Also, know that there are organizations founded specifically to help the single traveler. For example, Frommer/Pasmantier operates a Travel Club that publishes a quarterly newspaper containing several columns for readers—including a share-a-trip column used by travelers seeking companions to share expenses. There are many other organizations that will perform similar services for a small fee. Cruises and tours strictly for people traveling alone (no couples or families accepted) are run by Singleworld, 444 Madison Ave., New York, NY 10022 (tel. 212/758-2433). Singles may choose private accommodations or can share rooms if they wish.

A Table for One

In my guidebook research, I often must dine in restaurants alone. It is not nearly as much fun as dining with another, and it demands special precautions. I have a pleasant, somewhat gullible look about me, I never confess that I'm inspecting the restaurant for a guidebook, and so I frequently am asked to sit next to the kitchen doors, or the silverware racks, or the drafty doorway, or the cash register. Consequently, I am now a master at the steely look and the tense but even tone of voice which communicates to the hostess or maître d' that such a table is unacceptable. Unspoken, but looming large behind that statement, is the question, "Do you want my business, or not?" If so, then I had better get a more acceptable table.

The table by the kitchen door, or street door, or silverware clatter, is for customers who arrive later, when the restaurant has filled and when no alternative is available. They can then choose, on the basis of what's available, whether they wish to dine there or not. They can always wait for a better table to be vacated. This whole business has absolutely nothing to do with single or double.

It is proper and polite to accept a small table, well positioned, if you're dining alone. And if the little table is not horribly placed, why not? Asking for the very best table in the house, and asking for a decent table, are two completely different things. But if the management has lacked foresight and placed all the little tables in bad places, why should you be asked to give up your dining pleasure? They won't charge you any less because you're at a bad table. If things get tense, and they won't give you a decent table because it's larger, tell them you would be glad to have them seat someone else there as well. They then have no excuse for not giving in. Besides, this way you might meet someone interesting, which brings us to one of the great advantages of traveling alone.

Single Travel Is More Adventurous

Traveling in twos is more comfortable, but single travel is more adventurous. Traveling by yourself, you will definitely miss having someone along when that

exquisite scene comes into view, or the theater performance is superb, or the cuisine is fantastic. You will
also feel very alone when you miss your train, or
sprain an ankle, or walk back to your hotel at 1 a.m.,
or can't speak the local language. That is the way it is.
But you must dismiss the idea that single travel is any
less rewarding than traveling with others. It's not.
Besides, there are things you can do when you're
lonely.

The first is to write. Take time and set down your
experiences, or pour out your heart if that's what's
needed, into a diary or into a letter to someone you
love. The act of writing is cathartic, and more than
that, it is a very real way of enjoying that communica-
tion you lack. Although there is a time lag, you are in
fact sharing that beautiful view or that frustration over
the language with someone you love. And it is much
better to write than to telephone, because a phone call
catches a person unaware and unready. They may be
busy with something else, and it will certainly take
them some minutes (at what seems like $1,000,000
each) to come around and figure out who it is that's
calling, and from where, and why. Phone calls have
their place, of course. They are certainly a quick way
of reassuring yourself that your world still exists, and
that there are indeed familiar places and faces back
home, not just this strange, unintelligible, and horribly
indifferent foreign world.

If it's any comfort, couples traveling together also
feel homesick and lonely for familiar sights and
friends. It is just a bit more poignant when you're
alone.

But being alone has its compensations. The possibilities for new acquaintances, experiences, and adventures are virtually unlimited for the single traveler.
Even the most outgoing couples tend to insulate themselves against the world outside—that's where the
comfort of traveling together comes from. And if you

insulate yourself, you automatically limit the scope of your experiences.

Other ways to fend off loneliness are to spend part of your time making careful documentation of your trip. Draw up plans for a show of your photographs, or design (on paper) a recording you'd like to edit from live sound taping you've done. As you see the sights and explore new experiences, you will have a context and a purpose. Your show or recording can give people back home a comprehensive and balanced view of your travels. To make sure it does, you've got to go out of your way to get those extra photos which will fill gaps in the story. With an active purpose such as this, you forget at once the docile and disheartening role of passive sightseer. This is for real. You don't have to be going to some romantic spot or wild jet-set haven. Virtually any place in the world can be of interest to someone who hasn't been there, as each place has its own particular character, things to see and do, culinary quirks, and states of mind.

Loneliness Loves Company

The oldest cure for loneliness is also the simplest: other people. You must make yourself realize that there are many others in precisely your situation at this very moment, thinking your thoughts and feeling what you feel. And in this well-traveled world, there are probably several such people very close by. All you need to do is find them. Cafés, restaurants, pubs, promenades, lookouts, beaches—these are places people go to see and be seen. If you can just get up the courage to break the ice, you'll be able to dispel the sense of loneliness at once. How to do it?

The direct approach is usually best. Don't "scout" someone for too long before approaching them, or they'll think you're odd. When you notice someone who is probably your type, go right up and ask the time, or if they know a good restaurant nearby, or a good hotel, or what there is that's interesting to do. If it's obvious to the other person that you're only after conversation, the approach automatically becomes a compliment ("You look interesting—I'd like to find out more about you"). Don't be discouraged when you find that the person is waiting for someone else, or that they need to be alone, or that they don't speak your language. That's going to happen. Remember: you're looking for one of the numerous people who need just what you do—warmth and human conversation. When you meet them, you'll know it right away. They'll respond just the way you would if someone approached you. The eager response says it all.

The Single Woman

Yes, it is more difficult and dangerous for a woman traveling alone. (And I suppose it's no compensation to know that a man traveling alone will have more problems, too. Traveling in a couple is safer for *both* parties!) But it is done all the time with minimal risk, and you can do it too.

Many women have written to me regarding their experiences in Mediterranean countries, certainly among the world's most bothersome for single women. From most of these travelers the message was the same: common sense and awareness will suffice, paranoia is unnecessary. Unpleasant situations will appear. Most will contain no real danger. But all will affront your self-respect and independence as a capable, liberated woman. There may be little you can do about it, and the sense of annoyance and frustration may be very great.

The frustration may be greater because you don't have enough acquaintance with the local culture to interpret the signs and signals present in such a situation. What about the taxi driver who tells you to sit up front with him so you can see the view? Is he truly being nice? Will you miss something pretty? Or is it an improper suggestion? Do Mediterranean women get pinched and followed all the time like this? If not, how do they get rid of it?

The only way to find out is to learn more about the culture. This may not bring satisfaction in the form which you would prefer. You might find out that local custom demands a single woman should never go to the beach alone. Rather, she should go with other women friends, or with relatives, or in a mixed group. "But there's all that gorgeous beach out there, and I just want to be alone on it!" you say. That may simply be impossible. To the locals, it may appear as odd as someone undressing on a Fifth Avenue bus in summer. That, too, would be natural and seemingly rational— on a sweltering day—but it's just not done, and that's that. To a nudist from Polynesia, such a benighted attitude toward comfortable Fifth Avenue bus travel might be completely incomprehensible, but the Polynesian would have to conform to local custom in any case.

If you're going to be spending $2000 on a once-in-a-lifetime trip, make sure that you'll be getting what *you* want. Compare itineraries. . . . Then look at the other items. . . . Ask questions.

With time, many such problems can be solved in accordance with local custom. You will find others with whom to share the beach, or will attach yourself—for cultural purposes—to an existing beach group. You will learn such things as train-compartment etiquette, whereby an older couple may "adopt" a single woman for the duration of the trip, looking after her honor and dignity, and assuring her respectability. Their icy stares and even, well-chosen words will drive off any interlopers with questionable intentions—they're doing for you what they expect your parents would do for their daughter in your country.

Perhaps the fastest way to learn the customs of a country is to appeal to an older woman who lives there. Even if she doesn't speak your language, you can get your message across. The situations are universal and age-old, quickly comprehensible, and almost as quickly disposed of by someone familiar with them.

SPECIAL-INTEREST TRAVEL

What about something offbeat for your next trip? These days it is possible to sign up for a ten-day birdwatching trip to Iceland, a trek by dogsled across Greenland, a bicycle tour of the People's Republic of China, or a Land Rover expedition in Yemen. Shoot the rapids on the Euphrates in eastern Turkey, dive to inspect coral off the coast of Sinai, or hike through ancient kingdoms in the Himalayas. The world is open to you for exploration more than you may have realized!

Many of these special expeditions are expensive, however. Small groups, specially organized and accompanied by an experienced group leader, flying to infrequently visited places, are going to pay more than mass travelers on heavily traveled routes to mass-production resorts. You must select your adventure trip carefully, and perhaps ask for references from satisfied customers—if you're about to put out $1000 or $2000 for a few weeks' travel, you have a right to get opinions.

Consider any adventure destination and you'll find

several companies offering almost identical itineraries at very similar prices. For example, there are half a dozen or so companies operating safaris to East Africa. Don't just compare the overall price. If you're going to be spending $2000 on a once-in-a-lifetime trip, make sure that you will be getting what *you* want. Compare itineraries. One may visit several game parks; another may visit only one or two game parks and spend more time in Nairobi, let's say. Select the itinerary for you. Then look at the other items. Are all meals included in the price? Is transportation included both from the United States and within Africa? If you have any questions or doubts in your mind, query the company (it's always wise to get the facts in writing, by the way).

A useful tool in selecting adventure vacations is the *Adventure TravelGuide,* published by Ziff-Davis Publishing Company and distributed by Random House. The guide has over 500 pages of descriptions of adventure trips throughout the world, plus a handy reference list of clubs and associations (from the Balloon Federation of America to the National Speleological Society), and another of trip organizers. Currently, the guide sells for about $10. If it's not in your bookstore, write to Ziff-Davis at 1 Park Avenue, New York, NY 10016.

For the skiing enthusiast the best values are available to members of ski clubs. For information on clubs in the eastern United States, write to the **U.S. Ski Association,** P.O. Box 727, Brattleboro, VT 05301; for other regions, the **U.S. Ski Association Sports Division,** P.O. Box 100, Park City, UT 84060.

Another wonderful way to really get to know the country you're visiting and save money over a regular vacation is to study there. Many, many summer programs are offered the world over. For a comprehensive guide write for *Vacation Study Abroad* to the Communications Division, Institute of International Education, 809 United Nations Plaza, New York, NY

10017 (tel. 212/883-8200). It contains programs for all ages. If you do study abroad, the college or institution will often be willing to find you lodgings with a family for a very low price. This is one way to really capture the flavor and life of the people.

THE ULTIMATE TRAVEL VALUE: WORKING ABROAD

Early in his eventful life, Ernest Hemingway recognized that you never really know a place until you've earned your living there. Even staying a month in some city or country will tell you less than if you must get along on your own wages for a week.

Working while you travel is the most cost-effective travel of all. Stories abound of intrepid types who set out with $100 in their pockets and return two years later with $800, having traveled to the tip of South America, or across Asia, or 10,000 miles in North America. To do this, one needs a high tolerance for uncertainty and inconvenience, plus a lot of time. If your time is limited, you've got to plan well in advance.

The big hurdle to employment abroad is the work permit. As unemployment is a worldwide problem, no country wants foreigners to come in and take jobs from its own people. Usually you need exceptional qualifications—some skill that cannot be found in the native job market—to procure a work permit legally.

However, there are ways that you can work abroad, particularly if you just want to work a short time (several weeks or months). You can often get a job by talking to the boss, arranging for payment in cash, and setting up an excuse for why you're there. Scandinavian women easily get seasonal jobs as hostesses in Mediterranean resort bars and lounges; college-educated North Americans, Britons, and Australians can often support themselves by giving English lessons in non-English-speaking countries (talk to executives at banks and trading companies—they're the best prospects). Small-scale, short-term employment can be and is carried out this way.

There are lots of other possibilities, though. You can work for a voluntary service organization (they sometimes help pay expenses), or participate in an internship program, or work at an archeological dig, or lead a group of young people, or participate in the life of a kibbutz. To work on a kibbutz contact the Kibbutz Aliya Desk, Jewish Agency, 114 Fifth Ave., New York, NY 10011 (tel. 212/255-1338). The best source of information is the *Whole World Handbook* (New York: E. P. Dutton), put together by the Council on International Educational Exchange and sold in the travel sections of bookstores (about $6). Another good publication to get hold of is *Work-Study-Travel Abroad*, yours free by writing to the Director, Office of Congressional and Public Liaison, International Communications Agency, Washington, DC 20547.

If you're a student you can take advantage of the special arrangements made by the Council on International Educational Exchange for students to work abroad during vacations.

Travel Resource Listings

APPENDIX 1:
TOURIST OFFICES WORLDWIDE

Remember that many countries maintain information offices in numerous cities, so you might want to check your local telephone directory for a nearby office if you live in a major urban area. In any case, you can always get what you want from these East Coast (mostly New York City) addresses:

North America

BERMUDA: Bermuda Department of Tourism, Suite 646, 630 Fifth Avenue, New York, NY 10111; tel. 212/397-7700.

CANADA: Canadian Government Office of Tourism, 1251 Avenue of the Americas, Room 1030, New York, NY 10020; tel. 212/757-4917.

MEXICO: Mexican National Tourist Council, 405 Park Avenue, Suite 1002, New York, NY 10022; tel. 212/755-7212.

PUERTO RICO: Puerto Rico Tourism Company, 1290 Avenue of the Americas, Suite 3704, New York, NY 10104; tel. 212/541-6630.

Caribbean and West Indies

CARIBBEAN: Caribbean Tourism Association, 20 East 46th Street, New York, NY 10017; tel. 212/682-0435. Here's a list of the Association's member countries; an asterisk (*) indicates that the country also has its own tourism information office, listed below: Anguilla, Aruba*, Barbados*, Belize, Bonaire*, Cayman Islands*, Curaçao*, Dominica, Dominican Republic*, French West Indies* (Guadeloupe, Martinique, St. Barts, St. Martin), Haiti*, Jamaica*, Montserrat, Panama*, Puerto Rico, St. Kitts/Nevis*, St. Lucia*, St. Vincent and the Grenadines*, Surinam, Turks and Caicos Islands, U.S. Virgin Islands*, Venezuela*.

EASTERN CARIBBEAN: Eastern Caribbean Tourism Association, 220 East 42nd Street, New York, NY 10017; tel. 212/986-9370 (Members are: St. Kitts and Nevis).

ANGUILLA: (See Caribbean Tourism Association, above.)

ANTIGUA: Antigua Department of Tourism, 610 Fifth Avenue, New York, NY 10020; tel. 212/541-4117.

ARUBA: Aruba Tourist Bureau, 1270 Avenue of the Americas, New York, NY 10019; tel. 212/246-3030.

BAHAMA ISLANDS: Bahamas Tourist Office, 30 Rockefeller Plaza, New York, NY 10112; tel. 212/757-1611; or Bahamas News Bureau, 1345 Avenue of the Americas, New York, NY 10105; tel. 212/974-3156.

BARBADOS: Barbados Board of Tourism, 800 Second Avenue, New York, NY 10017; tel. 212/986-6516.

BELIZE: (See Caribbean Tourism Association, above.)

BONAIRE: Bonaire Tourist Information Office, 1466 Broadway, New York, NY 10036; tel. 212/869-2004.

BRITISH VIRGIN ISLANDS: British Virgin Islands Information Office, c/o John Scott Fones, Inc., 515 Madison Avenue, New York, NY 10022; tel. 212/371-6759.

CAYMAN ISLANDS: Cayman Islands Department of Tourism, 420 Lexington Avenue, New York, NY 10017; tel. 212/682-5582.

CURAÇAO: Curaçao Tourist Board, 685 Fifth Avenue, New York, NY 10022; tel. 212/751-8266.

DOMINICA: (See Caribbean Tourism Association, above.)

DOMINICAN REPUBLIC: Dominican Tourist Information Center, 485 Madison Avenue, New York, NY 10022; tel. 212/826-0750.

FRENCH WEST INDIES: French West Indies Tourist Board, 610 Fifth Avenue, New York, NY 10020; tel. 212/757-1125 (Members: Guadeloupe, Martinique, St. Barts, St. Martin).

GRENADA: Grenada Tourist Board, 141 East 44th Street, New York, NY 10017; tel. 212/687-9554.

GUADELOUPE: (See French West Indies, above.)

HAITI: Haiti Government Tourist Bureau, 1270 Avenue of the Americas, New York, NY 10020; tel. 212/757-3517.

JAMAICA: Jamaica Tourist Board, 866 Second Avenue, New York, NY 10017; tel. 212/688-7650.

MARTINIQUE: (See French West Indies, above.)

MONTSERRAT: (See Caribbean Tourism Association, above.)

PUERTO RICO: (See under North America, above.)

ST. KITTS AND NEVIS: (See under Eastern Caribbean Tourism Association, above.)

ST. LUCIA: St. Lucia Tourist Board, Suite 315, 41 East 42nd Street, New York, NY 10017; tel. 212/867-2950.

ST. MAARTEN/SABA/ST. EUSTATIUS: St. Maarten/Saba/St. Eustatius Information Office, Suite 1003, 25 West 39th Street, New York, NY 10018; tel. 212/840-6655.

ST. VINCENT AND THE GRENADINES: (See Caribbean Tourism Association, above.)

SURINAM: (See Caribbean Tourism Association, above.)

TRINIDAD AND TOBAGO: Trinidad & Tobago Tourist Board, 400 Madison Avenue, Suite 712, New York, NY 10017; tel. 212/838-7750.

TURKS AND CAICOS ISLANDS: (See Caribbean Tourism Association, above.)

U.S. VIRGIN ISLANDS: (See also British Virgin Islands, above.) U.S. Virgin Islands Division of Tourism, 1270 Avenue of the Americas, New York, NY 10020; tel. 212/582-4520.

Central and South America

ARGENTINA: Embassy of the Argentine Republic, 1600 New Hampshire Avenue, N.W., Washington, DC 20009; tel. 202/387-0705.

BOLIVIA: Embassy of Bolivia, 3014 Massachusetts Avenue, N.W., Washington, DC 20008; tel. 202/483-4410.

BRAZIL: Brazilian Tourism Office, 230 Park Avenue, Room 824, New York, NY 10169; tel. toll-free 800/221-1054.

CHILE: Embassy of Chile, 1732 Massachusetts Avenue, N.W., Washington, DC 20036; tel. 202/785-1746.

COLOMBIA: Colombian Government Tourism Office, 140 East 57th Street, New York, NY 10022; tel. 212/688-0151.

COSTA RICA: Costa Rican Tourist Board, 630 Fifth Avenue, Room 242, New York, NY 10111; tel. 212/245-6370.

ECUADOR: Ecuador Tourist Office, 1290 Avenue of the Americas, New York, NY 10104; tel. 212/247-8844.

EL SALVADOR: Embassy of El Salvador, 2308 California Avenue, N.W., Washington, DC 20008; tel. 202/265-3480.

GUATEMALA: Embassy of Guatemala, 2220 R Street, N.W., Washington, DC 20008; tel. 202/332-2865.

HONDURAS: Embassy of Honduras, 4301 Connecticut Avenue, N.W., Washington, DC 20008; tel. 202/966-7700.

NICARAGUA: Embassy of Nicaragua, 1627 New Hampshire Avenue, N.W., Washington, DC 20009; tel. 202/332-1643.

PANAMA: Panama Government Tourist Bureau, 630 Fifth Avenue, Suite 1414, New York, NY 10111; tel. 212/869-2530.

PARAGUAY: Embassy of Paraguay, 2400 Massachusetts Avenue, N.W., Washington, DC 20008; tel. 202/483-6960.

PERU: Peruvian Tourist Promotion Board, 1450 Coral Way, Suite 2, Miami, FL 33105; tel. 305/856-1498.

URUGUAY: Embassy of Uruguay, 1918 F Street, N.W., Washington, DC 20006; tel. 202/331-1313.

VENEZUELA: Venezuelan Government Tourist and Information Office, 450 Park Avenue, New York, NY 10022; tel. 212/355-1101.

Europe

AUSTRIA: Austrian National Tourist Office, 545 Fifth Avenue, New York, NY 10017; tel. 212/697-0651.

BELGIUM: Belgian National Tourist Office, 745 Fifth Avenue, New York, NY 10151; tel. 212/758-8130.

BULGARIA: Bulgarian Tourist Office, 50 East 42nd Street, New York, NY 10017; tel. 212/722-1110.

CZECHOSLOVAKIA: Czechoslovakia Travel Bureau, 10 East 40th Street, New York, NY 10016; tel. 212/689-9720.

FINLAND: Finland National Tourist Office, 75 Rockefeller Plaza, New York, NY 10019; tel. 212/582-2802 (use same address and phone for the other Scandinavian countries as well).

FRANCE: French Tourist Office, 610 Fifth Avenue, New York, NY 10020; tel. 212/757-1125.

GERMANY, FEDERAL REPUBLIC OF (WEST): German National Tourist Office, 747 Third Avenue, New York, NY 10017; tel. 212/308-3300.

GREAT BRITAIN: (See "United Kingdom," below.)

GREECE: Greek National Tourist Organization, 645 Fifth Avenue, New York, NY 10022; tel. 212/421-5777.

HOLLAND: (See "Netherlands," below.)

HUNGARY: IBUSZ Hungarian Travel Bureau, 630 Fifth Avenue, New York, NY 10111; tel. 212/582-7412.

ICELAND: Icelandic Tourist Office (same address and phone as Finland, above).

IRELAND: Irish Tourist Board, 590 Fifth Avenue, New York, NY 10036; tel. 212/869-5500.

ITALY: Italian Government Travel Office, 630 Fifth Avenue, New York, NY 10111; tel. 212/245-4822.

LUXEMBOURG: Luxembourg National Tourist Office, 801 Second Avenue, New York, NY 10017; tel. 212/370-9850.

NETHERLANDS: Netherlands National Tourist Office, 576 Fifth Avenue, New York, NY 10036; tel. 212/245-5320.

NORWAY: Norwegian National Tourist Office (same address and phone as Finland, above).

POLAND: Polish National Tourist Office, 500 Fifth Avenue, New York, NY 10110; tel. 212/391-0844.

PORTUGAL: Portuguese National Tourist Office, 548 Fifth Avenue, New York, NY 10036; tel. 212/354-4403.

RUMANIA: Rumanian National Tourist Office, 573 Third Avenue, New York, NY 10016; tel. 212/697-6971.

SPAIN: Spanish National Tourist Office, 665 Fifth Avenue, New York, NY 10022; tel. 212/759-8822.

SWEDEN: Swedish National Tourist Office (same address and phone as Finland, above).

SWITZERLAND: Swiss National Tourist Office, 608 Fifth Avenue, New York, NY 10020; tel. 212/757-5944.

TURKEY: Turkish Tourism Office, 821 United Nations Plaza, New York, NY 10017; tel. 212/687-2194.

UNITED KINGDOM: British Tourist Authority, 680 Fifth Avenue, New York, NY 10019; tel. 212/581-4700.

U.S.S.R.: Intourist, 630 Fifth Avenue, New York, NY 10111; tel. 212/757-3884.

YUGOSLAVIA: Yugoslav National Tourist Office, 630 Fifth Avenue, New York, NY 10111; tel. 212/757-2801.

Middle East and North Africa

EGYPT: Egyptian Tourist Office, 630 Fifth Avenue, New York, NY 10111; tel. 212/246-6960.

ISRAEL: Israel Government Tourist Office, 350 Fifth Avenue, New York, NY 10118; tel. 212/560-0650.

JORDAN: Jordan Information Bureau, 1701 K Street, N.W., Washington, DC 20006; tel. 202/659-3322.

MOROCCO: Moroccan National Tourist Office, 521 Fifth Avenue, New York, NY 10017; tel. 212/557-2520.

TUNISIA: Tunisian Information Office, 2408 Massachusetts Avenue, N.W., Washington, DC 20008; tel. 202/234-6650.

Africa South of the Sahara

KENYA: Kenya Tourist Office, 60 East 56th Street, New York, NY 10022; tel. 212/486-1300.

TANZANIA: Tanzania Embassy, 2010 Massachusetts Avenue, N.W., Washington, DC 20036; tel. 202/232-0501.

UNION OF SOUTH AFRICA: South African Tourist Organization, Suite 404, 610 Fifth Avenue, New York, NY 10020; tel. 212/245-3720.

Asia and Oceania

AUSTRALIA: Australian Tourist Commission, 630 Fifth Avenue, New York, NY 10111; tel. 212/489-7550.

CHINA, PEOPLE'S REPUBLIC: (No office yet; apply to a travel agent or any airline which flies to China.)

HONG KONG: Hong Kong Tourist Association, 548 Fifth Avenue, New York, NY 10036; tel. 212/869-5008.

INDIA: India Tourist Office, 30 Rockefeller Plaza, New York, NY 10112; tel. 212/586-4901.

INDONESIA: Directorate-General of Tourism of Indonesia, Suite 305, 323 Geary Street, San Francisco, CA 94102; tel. 415/981-3585.

JAPAN: Japan Tourist Organization, 630 Fifth Avenue, New York, NY 10111; tel. 212/757-5640.

KOREA: Korea National Tourism Corporation, Room 628, 460 Park Avenue, New York, NY 10022; tel. 212/688-7543.

MACAU: Macau Tourist Information Bureau, 60 East 42nd Street, New York, NY 10165; tel. 212/697-3694.

MALAYSIA: Malaysian Tourist Information Center, Suite 2148, 420 Lexington Avenue, New York, NY 10170; tel. 212/697-8995.

NEPAL: Royal Nepalese Embassy, 2131 LeRoy Place, N.W., Washington, D.C.; tel. 202/667-4550.

NEW ZEALAND: New Zealand Tourist Office, Suite 530, 630 Fifth Avenue, New York, NY 10111; tel. 212/586-0060.

PAPUA NEW GUINEA: Papua New Guinea Mission to the United Nations, 801 Second Avenue, New York, NY 10017; tel. 212/682-6447.

PHILIPPINES: Philippine Ministry of Tourism, 556 Fifth Avenue, New York, NY 10036; tel. 212/575-7915.

SINGAPORE: Singapore Tourist Promotion Board, 342 Madison Avenue, New York, NY 10173; tel. 212/687-0385.

SRI LANKA: Sri Lanka Tourist Board, Suite 308, 609 Fifth Avenue, New York, NY 10017; tel. 212/935-0369.

TAHITI: Tahiti Tourist Board, 366 Madison Avenue, New York, NY 10017; tel. 212/972-9444.

TAIWAN: Taiwan Coordination Council for North American Affairs, Suite 86155, One World Trade Center, New York, NY 10048; tel. 212/466-0691 or -0692.

THAILAND: Thai Tourist Office, Suite 2449, Five World Trade Center, New York, NY 10048; tel. 212/432-0433.

STATE AND CITY TOURISM OFFICES

The following is a selected list of state, territorial, and city tourism offices. Where a toll-free 800 number is available, it is given. However, the numbers are subject to change.

ALABAMA
Bureau of Publicity and
   Information
State Highway Building
Montgomery, AL 36130
(205/832-5510, or toll-free
   800/633-5761)

ALASKA
Alaska Division of Tourism
Pouch E
Juneau, AK 99811
(tel. 907/465-2010)

AMERICAN SAMOA
Director of the Office of
   Tourism
Pago Pago, American
   Samoa 96799

ARIZONA
Arizona Office of Tourism
1700 W. Washington
Phoenix, AZ 85007
(tel. 602/255-3618)

Phoenix
Phoenix & Valley of the Sun
   Convention and Visitor's
   Bureau
2701 E. Camelback Road
Phoenix, AZ 85016

Tucson
Visitor's Bureau
P.O. Box 991
Tucson, AZ 85702

ARKANSAS
Arkansas Department of
   Parks and Tourism
149 State Capitol Building
Little Rock, AR 72201
(tel. 501/371-7777, or
   toll-free 800/643-8383)

Hot Springs
Hot Springs Chamber of
   Commerce Convention
   and Visitors Division
P.O. Box 1500
Hot Springs, AR 71901

CALIFORNIA
Office of Visitor Services
Department of Economics
   and Business
   Development
1120 N. St.
Sacramento, CA 95814
(tel. 916/322-1396)

San Francisco
San Francisco Convention
   and Visitor's Bureau
1390 Market Street, Suite
   260
San Francisco, CA 94102

COLORADO
Office of Tourism
Colorado Division of
   Commerce and
   Development
133 Sherman St., Room 500
Denver, CO 80203
(tel. 303/866-2205)

CONNECTICUT
Tourism Promotion Service
Connecticut Department of
   Commerce
210 Washington St.
Hartford, CT 06106
(tel. 203/566-3385, or
   toll-free 800/243-1685)

DELAWARE
State Visitors Service
Division of Economic
   Development
630 State College Rd.
Dover, DE 19901
(tel. 302/736-4254).

**DISTRICT OF
   COLUMBIA**
Washington Convention and
   Visitors Association
Suite 250
1575 Eye Street, NW
Washington, DC 20005
(tel. 202/789-7000).

FLORIDA
Department of Commerce
   Visitors Inquiry
126 Van Buren Street
Tallahassee, FL 32301
(tel. 904/487-1462).

Miami
Miami Metro Department of
   Publicity & Tourism
499 Biscayne Blvd.
Miami, FL 33132

GEORGIA
Tourist Division
P.O. Box 1776
Atlanta, GA 30301
(tel. 404/656-3590, or
   toll-free 800/241-8444).

GUAM
Guam Visitors Bureau
P.O. Box 3520
Agana, GU 96910

HAWAII
Hawaii Visitors Bureau
2270 Kalakana Ave.
Suite 801
Honolulu, HI 96815
(tel. 808/923-1811).

IDAHO
Division of Tourism and
   Industrial Development
State Capitol Building,
   Room 108
Boise, ID 83720
(tel. 208/334-2470).

ILLINOIS
Office of Tourism
222 South College
Springfield, IL 62706
(tel. 217/782-7139).

Chicago
Convention and Tourism
    Bureau
McCormick Place on the
    Lake. Room 2050
Chicago, IL 60616
(tel. 312/225-5000).

INDIANA
Tourism Development
    Division
State House, Room 336
Indianapolis, IN 46204
(tel. 317/232-8860).

IOWA
Travel Development
    Division
250 Jewett Building
Des Moines, IA 50309
(tel. 515/281-3100/3679).

KANSAS
Tourist Division
Department of Economic
    Development
503 Kansas Ave.
6th Floor
Topeka, KS 66603
(tel. 913/296-3481).

KENTUCKY
Kentucky Department of
    Tourism
Capital Plaza Tower
Frankfort, KY 40601
(tel. 502/564-4930).

LOUISIANA
Louisiana Tourist
    Development
    Commission
P.O. Box 44291, Capitol
    Station
Baton Rouge, LA 70804
(tel. 504/342-4900).

New Orleans
Greater New Orleans
    Tourist & Convention
    Commission
334 Royal Street
New Orleans, LA 70130

MAINE
Maine Publicity Bureau
97 Winthrop Street
Hallowell, ME 04347
(tel. 207/289-2423).

MARYLAND
Division of Tourist
    Development
1748 Forest Drive
Annapolis, MD 21401
(tel. 301/269-3517, or
    toll-free 800/638-5252)
    (out of state)

MASSACHUSETTS
Division of Tourism
100 Cambridge Street
Boston, MA 02202
(tel. 617/727-3201).

Boston
Convention and Tourist
    Bureau, Inc.
Prudential Tower, Box 490
Boston, MA 02199
(tel. 617/536-4100).

MICHIGAN
Travel Bureau
Department of Commerce
P.O. Box 30226
Law Building
Lansing, MI 48909
(tel. 517/373-1195, or
    toll-free 800/248-5703)
    (out of state)

MINNESOTA
Tourism Division
480 Cedar St., Hanover
  Bldg.
St. Paul, MN 55101
(tel. 612/296-5029).

MISSISSIPPI
Department of Tourism and
  Development
P.O. Box 849
Jackson, MS 39205
(tel. 601/354-6715, or
  toll-free 800/647-2290).

MISSOURI
Missouri Division of
  Tourism
308 E. High St.
P.O. Box 1055
Jefferson City, MO 65102
(tel. 314/751-4133).

MONTANA
Travel Promotion Unit
Department of Commerce
1424 Ninth Avenue
Helena, MT 59620
(tel. 406/449-2654).

NEBRASKA
Division of Travel and
  Tourism
P.O. Box 94666, State
  Capitol
Lincoln, NB 68509
(tel. 402/471-3111).

NEVADA
Nevada Division of Tourism
Capitol Complex
1100 E. William Street
Suite 106
Carson City, NV 89710
(tel. 702/885-4322).

Las Vegas
Las Vegas Chamber of
  Commerce
2301 E. Sahara Aenue
Las Vegas, NV 89104
(tel. 702/457-4664).

NEW HAMPSHIRE
Office of Vacation Travel
P.O. Box 856
Concord, NH 03301
(tel. 603/271-2665).

NEW JERSEY
Division of Travel and
  Tourism
CN. 384
Trenton, NJ 08625
(tel. 609/292-2470).

Atlantic City
Greater Atlantic City
  Chamber of Commerce
10 Central Pier
Atlantic City, NJ 08401
(tel. 609/345-2251).

NEW MEXICO
Commerce and Industry
  Department
Travel Division
Bataan Memorial Building
Santa Fe, NM 87503
(tel. 505/827-5571, or
  toll-free 800/545-2040).

NEW YORK
Travel Bureau
New York State
99 Washington Avenue
Albany, NY 12245
(tel. 518/474-4116).

New York City
New York Convention and
   Visitor's Bureau
2 Columbus Circle
New York, NY 10019
(tel. 212/397-8222).

NORTH CAROLINA
Travel and Tourism Division
Department of Commerce
Box 25249
Raleigh, NC 27611
(tel. 919/733-4171).

NORTH DAKOTA
North Dakota Travel
   Division
1050 East Interstate Avenue
Bismarck, ND 58505
(tel. 701/224-2525, or
   toll-free 800/437-2077)
   (out of state)

OHIO
Ohio Office of Travel
P.O. Box 1001
Columbus, OH 43216
(tel. 614/466-8444).

OKLAHOMA
Tourism Promotion Division
505 Will Rogers Building
Oklahoma City, OK 73105
(tel. 405/521-2464).

OREGON
Travel Information Section
101 Transportation Building
Salem, OR 97310
(tel. 503/378-6309, or
   toll-free 800/547-4901).

PENNSYLVANIA
Bureau of Travel
   Development
416 Forum Building
Harrisburg, PA 17120
(tel. 717/787-5453, or
   toll-free 800/323-1717).

Philadelphia
Convention and Visitor's
   Bureau
1525 John F. Kennedy
   Blvd.
Philadelphia, PA 19102
(tel. 215/568-7255).

PUERTO RICO
Puerto Rico Tourism
   Development Company
P.O. Box 3072
Old San Juan Station
San Juan, PR 00913
(tel. 809/721-2400).

RHODE ISLAND
Department of Economic
   Development
Tourist Division
1 Weybosset Hill
Providence, RI 02903
(tel. 401/277-2601).

SOUTH CAROLINA
South Carolina Division of
   Tourism
Box 71
Columbia, SC 29202
(tel. 803/758-8735).

SOUTH DAKOTA
South Dakota Division of
  Tourism
221 South Central
Pierre, SD 57501
(tel. 605/773-3301, or
  toll-free 800/843-1390)
  (out of state)

TENNESSEE
Tennessee Tourist
  Development
P.O. Box 23170
Nashville, TN 37203
(tel. 615/741-2158).

TEXAS
Texas
P.O. Box 5064
Austin, TX 78763
(tel. 512/475-7123).

UTAH
Utah Travel Council
Council Hall, Capitol Hill
Salt Lake City, UT 84114
(tel. 801/533-5681).

VERMONT
Agency of Development
  and Community Affairs
Travel Division
61 Elm Street
Montpelier, VT 05602
(tel. 802/828-3236).

VIRGIN ISLANDS
Division of Tourism
P.O. Box 6400
St. Thomas, Virgin Islands
  00801
(tel. 809/774-2566).

VIRGINIA
Virginia State Travel
  Service
202 North Ninth Street
Richmond, VA 23219
(tel. 804/786-4484).

WASHINGTON
Washington State Dept. of
  Commerce and Economic
  Development
General Administration
  Bldg. G-3, Room 101
Olympia, WA 98504
(tel. 206/753-5630).

WASHINGTON, D.C.
See District of Columbia

WEST VIRGINIA
Travel Development
  Division
1900 Washington Street,
  East
Charleston, WV 25305
(tel. 304/348-2286).

WISCONSIN
Division of Tourism
Box 7605
Madison, WI 53707
(tel. 608/266-2161).

WYOMING
Wyoming Travel
  Commission
Frank Norris, Jr. Travel
  Center
Cheyenne, WY 82002
(tel. 307/777-7777, or toll
  free 800/443-2784).

APPENDIX 2:
A BED-AND-BREAKFAST SOURCE LIST

The bed-and-breakfast movement in North America is still in its early stages. In a few years, when we all have little computers in our homes, there will no doubt be a bed-and-breakfast data service.

Some of these information sources charge a small fee; others demand that you pay a membership fee and fill out a detailed application. Prices (indicated below if known) are subject to change, of course. It's a good idea to enclose a self-addressed stamped envelope with your request for information.

B & B AGENTS AND RESERVATIONS SERVICES

These agencies are usually linked to specific guest houses; they are not general agents for *all* guest houses. The agent may list places in Kansas City, and more in Texas, Oklahoma, Oregon, and Newfoundland, but none in other cities/states. So mail a request for information to each agency, including a self-addressed stamped envelope (a long one, please), and you'll get a brochure detailing the services of each.

International

The International Spareroom, Box 518, Solano Beach, CA 92075 (tel. 714/755-3194). Homes in nearly 40 states, Canada, and the United Kingdom. Two lists published: North America ($1), and U.K. ($1).

BB International, 1318 Southwest Troy St., Portland, OR 97219 (tel. toll-free 800/547-1463), has homes throughout the U.S., Canada, Scotland and England, Australia and New Zealand, and the U.S.

Virgin Islands. All bookings are made exclusively through travel agents, but you can call the toll-free number for information and availability. In Oregon, call 503/245-0440.

United States

Here are listings for the principal agencies, by state or area.

General

The Bed & Breakfast League, 20 Nassau Street, Princeton, NJ 08540, lists B & B's in major U.S. cities in its $3 directory. You must join the League ($45 single, $55 family, per year) to book, however. Write for details, the directory (send $3), and applications.

Alabama

Bed & Breakfast Birmingham, Box 31328, Birmingham, AL 35222 (tel. 205/591-6406). Lists more than a dozen homes in the Birmingham area.

Arizona

Bed and Breakfast in Arizona, 8433 N. Black Canyon, Suite 160, Phoenix, AZ 85021 (tel. 602/939-2180). Rooms in ranches and homes throughout Arizona for $30 double and up.

Mi Casa Su Casa, c/o Mrs. Ruth T. Young, Box 950, Tempe, AZ 85281 (tel. 602/990-0682). Rooms throughout the state.

California

San Francisco Private Room Service—American Family Inn, 2185-A Union Street, San Francisco, CA 94123 (tel. 415/931-3083). Rooms in the city and nearby for $35 to $45 double, with a two-night minimum.

Bed & Breakfast International, 151 Ardmore, Kensington, CA 94707 (tel. 415/525-4569). Rooms throughout southern California from $25 to $55 double; plus some rooms in Nevada, Washington, Hawaii, and New York City. Send SASE for brochure and application form.

Rent a Room International, 1032 Sea Lane, Corona del Mar, CA 92625 (tel. 714/640-2330). Rooms in southern California for about $35 double per night; three-night minimum stay. Send SASE.

Digs West, 8191 Crowley Circle, Buena Park, CA 90621 (tel. 714/739-1669). Includes accommodations in Orange County and around Disneyland. There's a $10 reservation fee.

Florida

Bed and Breakfast America, Box 3476, Clearwater Beach, FL 33515 (tel. 813/461-2924). Rooms and rental cottages throughout Florida in all price ranges; send $2 for information.

Bed & Breakfast Co., 1205 Mariposa Avenue No. 233, Miami, FL 33146 (tel. 305/661-3270). Double rooms in Miami for $30 to $45; free brochure.

Florida Suncoast Bed and Breakfast, Box 12, 119 Rosewood Dr., Palm Harbor, FL 33563 (tel. 813/734-5118). Homes in southwestern Florida in all price ranges. Send $3 for a list.

Georgia

Bed & Breakfast Atlanta, 1221 Fairview Road, N.E., Atlanta, GA 30306 (tel. 404/378-6026). Rooms in Atlanta for $25 to $35 double; free information.

Hawaii

Bed & Breakfast Hawaii, Box 449, Kapaa, HI 96746 (tel. 808/822-1582). Rooms on various islands for $20 to $35 double; send $5 for complete list. •

Massachusetts

Berkshire Bed and Breakfast Connection, c/o The Allens, 141 Newton Road, Springfield, MA 01118 (tel. 413/783-5111). Rooms in western Massachusetts for $20 to $30 double per night; free information.

House Guests, Cape Cod, Inc., 85 Hokum Rock Road RFD, Dennis, MA 02638 (tel. not available). Rooms and various offbeat accommodations from $20 to $60 double per night, depending on lodging and season. Free brochure with SASE.

New England Bed and Breakfast, Inc., 1045 Centre Street, Newton Centre, MA 02159 (tel. 617/498-9819). Rooms in the suburbs of Boston for $28 to $48 double; call anytime.

Pineapple Hospitality Bed & Breakfast, 384 Rodney French Blvd., New Bedford, MA 02744 (tel. 617/997-9952). Rooms in New Bedford, Plymouth, Cape Cod, Martha's Vineyard, and Boston suburbs for $25 to $40 double per night. Free brochure.

New York

E. P. Tobin's Bed and Breakfast, RD 2, Box 64, Rhinebeck, NY 12572 (tel. not available). For $2, you get a directory listing B & B's in the Hudson Valley, the Catskills, Mystic and Hartford (Conn.), Rhode Island, and Plymouth (Mass.)

New Yorkers at Home, 301 E. 60th St., New York, NY 10022 (tel. 212/838-7015). Lists more than 50 rooms in apartments and brownstones.

Urban Ventures, 322 Central Park West, New York, NY 10025 (tel. 212/662-1234). B & B rooms in New York City for $35 double and up. Free brochure.

Oregon

Northwest Bed & Breakfast, 7707 S. W. Locust St., Portland, OR 97223 (tel. 503/246-8366). Has listings that include Canada. There's a $15 single membership fee; $20 family.

Pennsylvania

Bed & Breakfast of Philadelphia, c/o Janet B. Mochel, Box 101, Oreland, PA 19075 (tel. 215/884-1084). Rooms in Philadelphia and Bucks County for $20 double and up; usually a two-night minimum. Free brochure.

Tennessee

Nashville Bed & Breakfast, c/o Betty Cordellos, Box 15651, Nashville, TN 37215 (tel. 615/292-2574). Rooms for $25 and up in the Nashville area; free brochure.

Vermont

American Bed & Breakfast, Box 983, St. Albans, VT 05478 (tel. 802/524-4731). Rooms in central and northern Vermont for $20 and up double. Free brochure.

Virginia

Guesthouses, c/o Sally Reger, 107 Bowlingwood Road, Charlottesville, VA 22903 (tel. 804/979-8327). Rooms in and around Charlottesville for $35 double per night. Free brochure.

Guesthouses Reservation Service, Box 5737, Charlottesville, VA 22903 (tel. 804/979-7264). Features Virginia homes and estate cottages.

Canada

British Columbia

Greater Vancouver Convention & Visitors Bureau, 650 Burrard Street, Vancouver, BC V6C 2L2 (tel. 604/682-2222). Write to the Convention and Visitors Bureau for a free list of B & B's in the Vancouver area, priced from $20 to $35 per night double.

Greater Victoria Visitor Information Centre, 812 Wharf Street, Victoria, BC V8W 1T3 (tel. 604/382-2127), lists several B & B's in Victoria; call or write.

Manitoba

Canadian B & B, 35 Pontiac Bay, Winnipeg, Manitoba R3K 0S6 (tel. not available), publishes a free list of B & B's in Winnipeg, Manitoba; Thunder Bay, Ontario; and Regina, Saskatchewan. Prices are low: $15 to $25 double.

New Brunswick

Tourism New Brunswick, Box 12345, Fredericton, NB E3B 5C3 (tel. 506/453-2377; toll-free in Canada, 800/561-0123). The provincial tourism authorities publish *New Brunswick Accommodations*, a free lodging directory which includes tourist homes. It's free—available from address above.

Nova Scotia

Department of Tourism, Box 130, Halifax, NS B3J 2M7 (tel. 902/423-5464; call 800/555-1212 for toll-free number). The provincial tourism authorities publish *Nova Scotia: Where to Stay, What to See, What to Do*, which includes tourist homes throughout the province. It's free.

Cape Breton Development Corporation, Box 1330, Sydney, NS B1P 6K3 (tel. 902/849-3276) administers the Cape Breton Bed & Breakfast Program, whereby dozens of tourist homes throughout Cape Breton Island provide breakfast as well as rooms for a set price (currently $18 double). Free list.

Nova Scotia Farm & Country Association, c/o Mrs. Sandra Houghton, RR 3, Centreville, Kings Co., NS B0P 1J0 (tel. 902/678-2329). Free list of B & B's throughout Nova Scotia.

Ontario

Ministry of Industry and Tourism, 5629 Falls Avenue, Niagara Falls, ON L2E 3P7 (tel. 416/684-2345), publishes a free list of B & B's in the vicinity of Niagara Falls, Ontario; prices are $16 double and up.

Canadian B & B, listed above under "Manitoba," lists B & B's in Thunder Bay, Ontario.

Toronto Bed & Breakfast, Box 86, Station T, Toronto, ON M6B 3Z9 (tel. not available), publishes a list of B & B's in Toronto for $1.

Ottawa Area Bed & Breakfast, Box 11263, Station H, Ottawa K2H 7T9 (tel. 613/820-0367, 828-9502), offers a free list of B & B's in Ottawa priced at $25 to $35 double.

Prince Edward Island

The Prince Edward Island Tourist Information Centre, Box 940, Charlottetown, P.E.I. (tel. 902/892-3457), distributes the official provincial *Accommodations Guide* for free. It lists tourist homes, B & B's, and self-catering ("efficiency") lodgings with full details and descriptions. *All* accommodations on the island are included.

Quebec

Montreal Bed & Breakfast/Maison d'accueil de Montreal, c/o Marian Kahn, 4692 Kent Avenue, Montreal, P.Q. H3W 1H1 (tel. 514/738-3859). For $1 they will send you a reservation application and descriptive folder. Rooms in Montreal are priced at $30 to $35 double.

Federation des agricotours du Quebec, 515 avenue Viger, 2e etage, Montreal, P.Q. H2L 2P2 (tel. 514/288-8090; toll-free in Quebec, 800/361-6196). The Federation arranges stays in farmhouses for about $20 per day, *all meals included*. Farms are located throughout the province; stays may be anywhere from one night to a month or more. Write or call the Federation, giving details of your requirements (when, where, how many, for how long).

Saskatchewan

Canadian B & B, listed above under "Manitoba," covers B & B's in the Regina area.

United Kingdom

General

Bed and Breakfast is so prevalent in England, Scotland, Wales and Ireland (both in the Republic and Northern Ireland) that listings are hardly necessary. Every city, town, and village seems to have B & B's. A sign, a question to a passerby, a local tourist office, or bulletin board provides your first lead. You call or ask; if they have no room, they will give you another address or telephone number. Armed with a pocketful of coins for the phone, a pad and pencil, and a half-hour or less, you'll find a room.

   If you want to make arrangements in advance, write to the local tourist office of the town you wish to visit, or use one of the services listed below.

England and Scotland

At Home in England, 10 West 86th Street, New York, NY 10024 (tel. 212/595-2087). This service matches up guests and hosts in London, the rest of England, and Scotland; three-night minimum in Scotland and the English countryside, five-night minimum in London. Prices for rooms are $40 to $54 single, $66 to $92 double (not exactly cheap: a normal B & B in, say, Stratford-on-Avon or Oxford will cost $40 double).

The International Spareroom, listed above under "International," includes rooms in the U.K., as does BB International.

Once you are in the U.K., many Tourist Information Centres (TIC's), located throughout the country, will Book-A-Bed-Ahead, that is, find you a B & B room in the next town you plan to visit, for a fee of $3 or $4. Most will be glad to find you a B & B room in their own town for free, or for a minimal fee.

Mexico

Posada Mexico, Apartado 21-C, Cuernavaca, Morelos, Mexico (tel. 731-2-1367 or 731-2-6419) organizes bed-and-breakfast stays in Cordoba, Cuernavaca, Guadalajara, Guanajuato, Jalapa, Merida, Mexico City, Oaxaca, Taxco, and Veracruz. Charges are about $30 double. In Mexico this price is no fantastic bargain, but rather a moderate price for a homey accommodation that's more sympathetic than a hotel.

APPENDIX 3: BUDGET MOTEL CHAINS

Best Value Inns
1115 East Hennepin
Avenue
Minneapolis, MN 55414
(Toll-free res: 800/
328-5511; in MN 800/
462-5355)

A group of individual motels, privately run, throughout the U.S. which band together to produce a common directory and toll-free reservations service. Double rooms cost about $20 to $30.

Budget Host Inns
2601 Jacksboro Hwy.
Caravan Suite 202
P.O. Box 10656
Fort Worth, TX 76114

Budget Host Inns are independent budget motels that band together to publish a directory and maintain standards. You'll find them in 31 states, and the province of British Columbia. Double rooms cost about $26 to $36.

California 6/
Western 6 Motels
1156 So. 7th Avenue
Hacienda Heights, CA
91745
(tel: 213/961-1681)

California 6 motels (in California), and Western 6 or Western $aver motels in Washington, Oregon, Nevada, Arizona, New Mexico, and Texas are very comfortable—almost luxurious—some with swimming pools and family suites, all with low prices.

Chalet Susse International
Two Progress Avenue
Nashua, NH 03060
(Toll-free res:
800/258-1980)

Susse Chalet Motor Lodges and Inns are in New England, Ohio, Illinois, and Florida. Lodgings have swimming pools, TVs, air conditioning, coin-op laundries; credit cards accepted. Rooms cost $24 to $30 double.

Days Inns of America, Inc.
2751 Buford Hwy. N.E.
Atlanta, GA 30324
(Toll-free res: call
    800/555-1212 for correct
    toll-free number)

A large number of clean, modern no-frills motels concentrated in the southeastern states. Double rates from $22 to $32. Credit cards accepted.

Econ-o-Inn of America, Inc.
P.O. Box 2603
Fargo, ND 58108
(Toll-free res:
    800/238-2552)

Seven motels in North Dakota, two more in South Dakota and Minnesota. Rates from $20 to $28 double.

Econo-Travel Motor Hotel Corp.
20 Koger Executive Center
P.O. Box 12188
Norfolk, VA 23502
(Toll-free res:
    800/446-6900, or
    800/446-8134; in Canada,
    800/267-9170)

Econo-Travel Motor Hotels and EconoLodges are scattered throughout the U.S. in over 100 locations. Greatest concentrations are in Florida, North and South Carolina, and Virginia. Double rooms cost $22 to $30, and facilities may include color TV, pool, and restaurants. Anyone over 55 can apply for a 10% discount; some motels give seventh night for free; children under 12 stay free in their parents' room. Major credit cards accepted.

Guest Quarters, Inc.
2550 M St., N.W.
Washington, DC 20037
(Toll-free res:
    800/424-2900)

These lodgings offer luxury studio, one- and two-bedroom suites with fully equipped kitchenettes, and hotel maid service. Rates are competitive with luxury hotels, but you get more space and convenience here. Locations: Washington, D.C. (and Alexandria, Va.); Atlanta, Houston, and Greensboro, N.C.

Rates: $120 double in Washington for a one-bedroom suite; special low weekend rates for up to four people.

Interstate Inns
P.O. Box 760
Kimball, NB 69145
(tel: 308/235-4616)

Inns in Nebraska, Colorado, Wyoming, Kansas, Oklahoma, and Iowa, with doubles priced 25% or more below the luxury chains. Their "directory" is a one-dollar-off bonus coupon (you'll receive two). Credit cards accepted.

La Quinta Motor Inns, Inc.
P.O. Box 32064
San Antonio, TX 78216
(Toll-free res:
   800/531-5900; in Texas,
   800/292-5200)

Pronounced "La-KEEN-tah," these inns are in 25 states in the Midwest, South, and Southwest, especially Texas. Almost luxurious doubles cost from $28 to $40, depending on location. Credit cards accepted.

Motel 6, Inc.
51 Hitchcock Way
Santa Barbara, CA 93105

One of the oldest and best budget chains, Motel 6 rooms used to cost $6. Now they're $17 for two; a TV can be rented for 75¢ a day. Clean, modern, comfortable, often with a pool, Motel 6s are in 39 states (especially California). *No credit cards*. Cash in advance for the room (keeps prices low).

Regal 8 Inns
P.O. Box 1268
Mt. Vernon, IL 62864

Modern rooms with color TV, double beds; swimming pools. In 19 states, especially Illinois and Indiana. Rooms cost $21 to $30 for two people.

Super 8 Motels
P.O. Box 1456
Aberdeen, SD 57401
(Toll-free res:
  800/843-1991)

A chain of 115 budget motels scattered throughout the U.S., mostly in the North Central states, charging $20 to $30 double. Credit cards accepted; several discount plans. Many rooms for handicapped.

Thr-rift Inns, Ltd.
P.O. Box 2699
Newport News, VA 23602
(Toll-free res:
800/446-1066)

Four motels in Virginia and Maryland priced at $22 to $40 double, depending on location and season.

Index

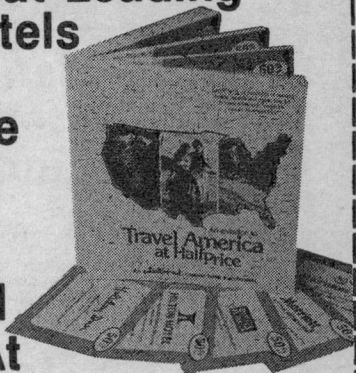